LET ME BE FRANK

A BOOK ABOUT WOMEN WHO DRESSED LIKE MEN TO DO SHIT THEY WEREN'T SUPPOSED TO DO

TRACY DAWSON

ILLUSTRATIONS BY TINA BERNING

HARPER DESIGN

An Imprint of HarperCollins Publishers

CONTENTS

INTRODUCTION

We all know that history books were written by the people who held the power and the pen—old white dudes. A lot of people got left off the page. Subsequently, they were left out of curriculums, out of oral histories, and out of dope biopics that definitely should have been made about them. *Let Me Be Frank* is filled with women from 1478 BCE to today who were told, "No, you can't do that. You can't go there or be that because you are a woman." To which these women all replied, "Yeah, no, FUCK THAT."

Some of them had a calling. They couldn't NOT do the thing, like practice medicine or play sports. Some were gifted or even geniuses. And some of them were just regular women, like me, trying to do their thing. Like I say to my dog sometimes when he's bugging me an hour early for his dinner and I'm trying to meet a deadline, "Can you just let me live?"

I was compelled to write this book. There is no other way to describe it. In 2013, I was a newish-to-America TV writer in Hollywood by way of

Toronto, taking meetings during "staffing season" with different producers, networks, and studios, hoping to land my first American job. We call it the Water Bottle Tour, and many writers hate it. But me? I love free water (it's the new gold!) and I love meetings. Each meeting represents potential and possibility. I think this attitude shows both my true and strong belief in my talents and that I have something everyone who survives in show business must possess: a healthy dose of delusion.

So, there I was on Water Bottle Tour 2013. I met with an exec at a major studio who asked me which of their new shows I might be interested in writing on. When I told her, she replied, plainly, that none of the shows I had mentioned had any "female needs." I just want to pause here to let that marinate for a second. She said that none of the shows I mentioned had any *female needs*. And that, my friends, is when my vision blurred and I passed out. Not really, no. That is when I learned that in her eyes (and maybe the industry's eyes) I was not a comedy writer with a flair for great dialogue (which I am). No. I was a Female Writer, and I was not going to be judged on my merits or jokes. There were jobs open that I was not eligible for . . . because I had boobs.

After I picked my mouth up off the floor and left her office, my dignity in tatters, wondering if this exec had ever told an African American writer that their shows didn't have any "Black needs" (and if she didn't say it, you *know* she's probably thought it), I went home to my very small apartment and thought, Well, fuck. I'm not super femme-y. I don't have cheekbones to speak of or much of a bosom. I wondered what actions could be taken. Could I reinvent myself? After all, everyone thought I was a boy when I was little . . . then would I be allowed to write some fucking jokes? That is when the fury set in. I paced around my living room like a caged animal. So, women are specialty items, huh? Added for flavoring? God forbid a woman is seen as simply a writer who can write for any multitude of voices and characters. Oh, no, that was *men's* work, I was being told. I was "niche," a fancy donut in a box of regular raised, and you only get ONE of those in a dozen. No, ma'am, so sorry, but we can't read and consider you based on how excellent your story, dialogue, and jokes are . . . they have been eclipsed by your small but dense breasts.

That moment in the exec's office was the beginning of this book. I was angry. Hell, I'm still angry. While I didn't seriously consider transforming into the man version of myself so I could get a job on a sitcom, I did think about it. Soon afterward, an article on *Jezebel* by Catherine Nichols caught my eye as it made the rounds online. In the article, entitled "Homme de Plume: What I Learned Sending My Novel Out Under a Male Name," Nichols wrote about how she sent out query letters and the first ten pages of her novel to literary agents using her real (female) name. After a dismal response, she sent it out again with a fake (male) name: George. Everything else remained the same about her submission. All told, almost nine times the number of agents asked to read the full manuscript when she submitted using a male name. Nichols writes:

> *Most of the agents only heard from one or the other of us, but I did overlap a little. One who sent me a form rejection as Catherine not only wanted to read George's book, but instead of rejecting it asked if he could send it along to a more senior agent. Even George's rejections were polite and warm on a level that would have meant everything to me, except that they weren't to the real me. George's work was "clever," "well-constructed" and "exciting." No one mentioned his sentences being lyrical or whether his main characters were feisty.*

I started to think of all the women throughout history who have disguised themselves as men or adopted a male pseudonym to gain access, get ahead, survive, thrive, be listened to, be *allowed* to . . . to embrace their true calling or to be taken seriously.

Look, here's the thing. I will never get over the 2016 presidential election. If you are reading this in 2180 and I'm dead in the ground, I'm still not over it. And not because I'm obsessed with Hillary Clinton. It's not about Clinton—it's about *me* and it's about women. We all lived through the buffoon who's never read a book triumphing over the Beyond Capable Woman. Don't get me wrong, even if the buffoon had lost, his numbers still would have been good because ours is a broken country that has never addressed its original sin, much like the bodies beneath the house in the film *Poltergeist*. But watching the Beyond Capable Woman lose does something to you. It burrows deep beneath your skin and settles there like a cancer. You may be accomplished, you may be qualified, but the message received since time immemorial is: No, not for you. Sorry, ladies. You may be exceptional but NOT. FOR. YOU.

Some of the women in this book are trailblazers, some are sociopaths, all are rule breakers. In fact, they are rule breakers in two ways: by doing the thing they were not supposed to do, and then by doing something women are definitely not supposed to do: *put themselves first.*

My focus in this book is on women who dressed as men to gain access and opportunity, not on gender identity. When it comes to historical figures, sometimes it is difficult to separate choices made for access or survival from those regarding gender identity. Caution is always required when applying modern language to historical figures. I'm not here to erase or oversimplify anyone's story. I don't have all the answers, but sometimes historians and scholars like to write like they do. I love facts and history, but I also love questions! I *live* in the questions, because staying open and curious most definitely keeps you young. This book is not about gender identity, but know that I am rigorous in my sensitivity and my commitment to inclusion.

Since I began my research for this book, I have been reminded of how many bullshit falsehoods I have told myself over the years, in conjunction with stories that show business, or the media, or advertisements, or the patriarchy have told me about who I am, what I am capable of, or what a woman is or is not. It's exhausting and maddening. Luckily, I have come to discover that I am deeply in love with myself and think I'm kinda the shit. I hope the women in this book will inspire you to feel the same.

Each of these stories celebrates the creativity and depth of ingenuity that my community and I have boldly harnessed in the face of the patriarchy's fucked-up desire to control and oppress us. Above all, it shows that female will, and the will of all those who have been othered, knows no boundaries. We get knocked down, but we keep getting up. We always GET. UP.

HANNAH SNELL

The story goes that in 1750, in a tavern in Gravesend, England, Royal Marine James Gray confessed to his fellow officers that he had something prettyyyy big to tell them. I bet you can guess what that was, but let's start at the beginning.

Upon being abandoned by her philandering husband whilst heavily pregnant, Hannah Snell decided to take charge of her own destiny. All she had to do was, you know, have a baby first. Sadly, like many infants born in the eighteenth century, her baby didn't survive a year. While Hannah licked her wounds and nursed her heartbreak, she realized she could maybe actually do something about the fuckwit who had abandoned her and her unborn child. She became determined to track the bastard down. Now, if

I had been friends with Hannah, that is not the advice I would have given her. I tried to make too many lovers stay in my youth and it is NOT a good look. But I choose to think she wanted to find the lobcock to give him shit, not because she was so lovesick and lost without him. In those days, a woman of Hannah's station would need to either reacquire the old husband or think about remarrying, and it sounds as if she was like, "Um, I am NOT starting from scratch with a new one." (Lobcock, by the way, is an eighteenth-century insult I'm rather fond of: a large, flaccid penis. Mmmm.) There is no definitive explanation as to what Hannah's reasoning was in wanting to track down her ex, but it's no surprise that there are a few scholars out there who paint the picture that Hannah loved him sooooo much she felt she couldn't live without him. The guy who upped and bounced in the middle of her third trimester. That guy. I'm feeling strongly that it was much more about finances and her, I don't know, *survival*, but let's move on.

When Hannah heard that her husband had joined the military, her first thought was not, "Oh well, guess that's that." Nope, her much more amazing idea was, "Oh, cool, I will go to there and I will get him." She immediately understood that the best way to search for the hubs was to pass herself off as a man, which would afford her a freedom of movement she wouldn't have as a woman. Hannah, clearly not one for dillydallying, jumped right in and cut off her hair, borrowed the clothing and identity of her brother-in-law James Gray, and set off to join the British Army and find her sonofabitch spouse. Allow me to work in calling her ex a fartleberry here, the eighteenth-century term for "excrement hanging about the anus." Hanging about. Ha. Like the doo-doo's just chilling outside the butthole, seeing if it can bum a smoke off someone. I'm sorry, I promise I'm not inebriated.

Let's just think about this for a moment. Hannah's baby has died. The poor woman doesn't just take a minute for some self-care, a notion that certainly would have been scoffed at—there were no turmeric golden milk lattes on offer in Worcester in those days. No, she sets her mind on a plan, gets hold of some men's clothes, and JOINS THE MILITARY to track down her husband. Look, I'm not saying she made the *healthiest* choices, but hell, when I was in my twenties it took me dating THREE dudes in a row who were twelve to seventeen years older than me before I realized I had daddy issues, so who am I to judge?

Hannah soon learned that her no-good husband—let's go ahead and call him a beard splitter ("a man much given to wenching")—had been found guilty of murder and was sentenced to death. Can you say "rejection is protection," Hannah? Times being what they were, and this bitch being the coolest chick in Coventry, our friend "James Gray" decided to stick with her "live as a dude and be a soldier" plan. Maybe she had few options. Maybe that was the best way for her to escape extreme poverty. And maybe, just maybe, she *liked* being a soldier, because, all told, she sounds like she was damn good at it.

Hannah-as-James became a soldier in the Sixth Regiment of Foot and was stationed in Carlisle during the Jacobite rebellion in Scotland. During this time Hannah was trained in military drills and the use of firearms. However, after she prevented a sergeant from raping a local girl (How to Be an Ally 101), she was sentenced to six hundred lashes of the whip for "neglect of duty." Yes, because your duty as an officer and a gentleman was to let your superior commit sexual assault. Cool, cool, cool.

No surprise, Snell covered her whipped flanks with whatever the eighteenth-century version of Neosporin was and got the hell out of Dodge. Still living as James Gray and having gotten used to that three-squares-a-day military lifestyle, Hannah went on to join the Royal Marines and set sail for India on HMS *Swallow*. In 1748, she fought in the Siege of Pondicherry, where she reportedly killed several Frenchmen before being wounded. She suffered a musket shot to the groin but quickly "operated" on herself, digging the musket balls out of her own crotch so that the medic would not discover that she was a person with an innie, not an outie. I mean . . . *wow*.

At a pub one night in 1750, after returning from battle and perhaps after a bit too much ale, Hannah decided to come clean to her fellow marines and exclaimed, "Lads, I'm a lady!" Shockingly, they were cool about it. They respected and supported Hannah, having fought side by side with her and having witnessed her skill and bravery. With their encouragement, Hannah requested, and was granted, a military pension and was honorably discharged from the army. (That is my favorite part of the story. I love these guys!) Hannah's exploits soon became popular gossip, and, finding her financial situation to be once again rather precarious, she eventually sold her story to the London bookseller Robert Walker, who published it with the title *The Female Soldier; or, The Surprising Life and Adventures of Hannah Snell* (1750). As a sensational book publicity tie-in, Hannah began performing a one-woman show around town, most notably at Sadler's Wells Theatre in the Clerkenwell area of London. Hannah sang ballads and told of her adventures, but perhaps most thrilling to the audience was when she appeared in military (male) garb and performed traditional musket drills.

Hannah retired to Wapping, where she opened a pub called The Female Warrior. The sign hanging out front displayed a portrait of her in "female" dress on one side and in marine uniform on the other, with the inscription "The Widow in Masquerade." We always knew this broad was enterprising, amirite?

She lived for another forty years, married twice more, and raised two sons. Sadly, Hannah's story concludes with her son George committing her to Bethlem Hospital in Lambeth—yes, the notorious Bedlam for the mentally disturbed—where she spent her final days. It was, however, gratifying

THE WIDOW IN MASQUERADE

to learn that Hannah's final request to be buried at the Royal Chelsea Hospital, where old military men see out their days, was granted, and it is where she rests today.

The next time someone wants to break up with you or straight up abandon your ass, maybe think of Hannah Snell and the fact that being dumped was the best thing that ever happened to her, inspiring her to set off on the biggest adventure of her damn life. She had to step up and take care of herself at a time when women were expected to let the man be in charge of . . . well, everything. We love you, Hannah Snell. I hereby deem you Patron Saint of the Dumped but Undaunted.

RENA "RUSTY" KANOKOGI

Born Rena Glickman in Brooklyn, Rusty Kanokogi was a redheaded fire-cracker from the moment she was born, in 1935, to the time of her demise, in late 2009. As early as age seven, Rena was a bit of a hustler, taking odd jobs anywhere she could get them. She found a sense of belonging amongst society's rejects: the freaks, hustlers, and barkers of the Coney Island under-world. By adolescence she was the head of a street gang called the Apaches and was given the nickname "Rusty" after a local dog, which I'm guessing involved a neighborhood child who began smoking at age seven observing that Rena and said dog had the same hair color, and thus a nickname was born.

According to a 1986 profile in *Sports Illustrated*, Rusty's hero was her brother, Charles, who spent hours squeezing handgrips and doing push-ups and then admiring his body in the mirror. Neglected at home, Rusty was a kid looking for attention and trouble. She started using her brother's exercise gadgets and working out. She was the biggest—and was determined to be the toughest—girl in her neighborhood.

Rusty began to derive her self-worth from being a fighter and a protector. As *Sports Illustrated* tells it, "She got a twelve-stitch knife wound on her wrist while preventing an armed robbery in a restaurant. She jumped in between a sailor and a soldier brawling at a hotel dance and was pitched off a balcony, suffering a badly sprained back" that pained her for the rest of her life. Rusty was troubled, feeling she didn't fit in with most men, who wanted her to be typically feminine, which to her meant "weak," or with women, who she felt resented her for rejecting "femininity." Rusty was at sea.

In 1955, when she was twenty years old, a neighborhood friend, perhaps sensing that she needed a place to channel her troubled energy, introduced her to judo. She fell in love instantly. She convinced the judo instructor at her local YMCA to let her join his class of forty men. "I didn't go for self-defense," Rusty confessed. "I did it to calm down." I interpret that as using judo and the focus, energy, and camaraderie of training to help with mental health issues. While I can't find anything identifying Rusty as someone who battled anxiety or depression, feeling the need *to calm down* just says so much about potential internal turmoil. Maybe this judo class was also the pseudo family she yearned for, a place to belong. And, finally, she *did* belong.

Rusty was the first one to show up at class and the last one to leave. She practiced moves on subway platforms, and she even began to apply specific judo moves to her still-fervent need to be the enforcer and protector. One day while riding the subway, "she stopped exercising long enough to notice a pervert exposing himself on the train. She drove her knee into his chin, pinned his arm behind his back, jerked the emergency stop cord and took him to the police station still unzipped." I'm . . . I'm . . . *in love.*

Some heroes wear capes, some have ladies' size 10½ EEE feet and a left baby toe that has been broken thirteen times. Despite her natural affinity for judo, there was a shitty kicker—Rusty couldn't compete. I mean, she could barely train. Why? Because she was a woman.

Many years later, Rusty identified the one moment in her life that changed everything, the thing that would inevitably lead to her being deemed the Mother of Women's Judo. In 1959, twenty-four-year-old Rena decided to cut off her hair and tape down her breasts to compete with her all-male club in the New York State YMCA championships judo tournament. Before her match, her coach pulled her aside and cautioned her, "Don't attract any attention to yourself. Just pull a draw." As in, don't be too good, just be okay. (That's what we call reverse-Miyagi-ing for all you *Karate Kid* fans.) But skilled and fiery Rusty couldn't tamp down her greatness. She triumphed in her weight division! When it came time to collect her medal after winning her bout, the suspicious tournament organizer asked her if she was a girl. She nodded, and he stripped her of her medal right then and there.

This moment of injustice sparked something in Rusty that would change not only her life but the lives of countless women and the sport of judo itself. In an article in the *New York Times* written toward the end of her life, Rusty recalled when the official asked her if she was female: "Had I said no, I don't think women's judo would have been in the Olympics. It instilled a feeling in me that no woman should have to go through this again." It set her advocacy in motion. She was in for a hell of a fight. But this was a woman who was known to do leg squats on the D train from Brooklyn to Manhattan each morning. She was not going to back down quietly.

In 1962, at age twenty-seven, Rusty felt so limited in how she was able to train in the United States that she moved to Japan. There, women had been training in judo since the 1920s in female-only groups. And guess what? Soon after joining the women's group, she pulverized each of her

teammates. She was so out of their league there was only one solution: for the first time in history, a woman (my girl Rusty!) was permitted to train with the men at the Kodokan.

She not only found a place to train and acceptance in Japan but also met her soul mate, Ryohei Kanokogi, a powerful black belt in judo over whom she towered. At one point, hot-tempered Rusty broke her hand fighting with a woman in a barroom bathroom for making a disparaging remark about the Japanese. It was then that she knew she had found her true love, because instead of scolding her, her future husband advised, "When you punch head, always wrap handkerchief around hand." They were married in 1964 by a Buddhist priest in New York City.

By all accounts, Rusty was a funny, brash, loudmouthed pain in the ass. *Well, thank God.* A driving force behind the battle for Title IX, she spent decades fighting for public recognition of women's judo, even going so far as to mortgage her house to sponsor the first women's judo championship, at Madison Square Garden in 1980. She got into more than one screaming match with officials about it and eventually threatened to sue the Olympic Committee in 1988 to force them to include women's judo. She went on to coach the women's Olympic team that year. Can you say TITAN?

In a statement issued after her death, fellow pioneer and Women's Sports Foundation founder Billie Jean King said, "Nothing thrilled Rusty more than helping others—especially children. She said that helping a child who thinks he or she can't do something and then showing them that they CAN DO IT, was one of the greatest feelings in her life."

Rena "Rusty" Kanokogi was a leader, a teacher, a sensei. The Japanese word *sensei* literally means "one who has gone before"—a fitting title for this trailblazer. Rusty was the first American woman to earn a seventh-degree black belt. She was awarded the Japanese Order of the Rising Sun in 2008 and was buried in the Kanokogi family tomb with the epitaph "American Samurai." In August 2009, three months before her death and fifty years after she won it, the YMCA re-awarded her the gold medal that had been stripped from her in that 1959 match.

Domo arigato, sensei.

ELLEN CRAFT

The escape from slavery of Ellen Craft, a light-skinned mixed-race woman from Georgia, and her husband, William Craft, is known as the most ingenious in fugitive slave history—even more amazing than that of Henry "Box" Brown, who escaped by mailing himself in a wooden crate to abolitionists in Philadelphia in 1849.

Not much is known about Ellen's mother, Maria. She is described, like her daughter, as a light-skinned mixed-race slave. This image so innocently describes what can only mean a horrifying lineage of rape and bondage. Ellen was born into slavery when her mother became pregnant by her enslaver, Major James Smith, a lawyer, surveyor, and one of the richest men in central Georgia. Because of her parentage, Ellen was frequently mistaken for white. Major Smith's wife abhorred Ellen's presence—she was a constant reminder of his sexual treachery, since Ellen looked more like one of her own children than the child of a slave. For this reason, Ellen was sent away at age eleven, given as a wedding gift to another household, as if it were totally normal to give a little girl, a human being, as a GIFT.

So, Ellen was sent away as a child, which is horrifying, and that new household was where she would eventually cross paths with William Craft. William and Ellen fell in love, and with the permission of their respective "owners," they married. They knew in their hearts that they did not want to start a family while in bondage, Ellen knowing from experience that her children could be taken from her at any moment. This deep desire to have children—*free* children—led to a steely-eyed focus on how they might escape.

At its peak, nearly one thousand slaves per year escaped using the Underground Railroad, which was a network of Black and white abolitionists who, between the late eighteenth century and the end of the Civil War, helped fugitive slaves escape to freedom. The Underground Railroad used a series of routes and safe houses to assist fugitive slaves in reaching free states in the North and Canada.

Side note: Until 1821, fugitive slaves also escaped to Spanish Florida, which was Florida but, like, owned and operated by Spain. Florida became a United States territory in 1821. One of the main reasons Florida was purchased by the United States was to end its function as a haven for escaped slaves. That's how much these maniacs were addicted to the atrocity of owning other humans. THEY BOUGHT CRAZY-ASS FLORIDA.

Utilizing the Underground Railroad meant relying on the help of others and literally running to freedom, often in the dead of night. There are few stories as incredible as William and Ellen's, for they devised a plan and undertook their escape all by themselves, and they did not run using their own identities . . . they did not "run" at all. In 1848, when Ellen was twenty-two, she and William decided to flee in plain sight. Knowing that slaveholders could take their slaves to any state, even free ones, fair-skinned Ellen would pose as an infirm white plantation owner and William would pretend to be her enslaved valet, traveling north to Philadelphia.

William was enslaved by a man who permitted him to work as a carpenter on the side and keep some of his earnings. He used that money to buy men's clothes for Ellen. William went to different shops, at odd times of the day, and purchased the makings of Ellen's disguise piece by piece. The night before their escape, William cut his wife's hair to add to her masculine appearance. In the Crafts' memoir, *Running a Thousand Miles for Freedom* (1860), William tells us: "We sat up all night discussing the plan, and making preparations. Just before the time arrived, in the morning, for us to leave, I cut off my wife's hair square at the back of the head, and got her to dress in the disguise and stand out on the floor. I found that she made a most respectable looking gentleman."

Ellen had painstakingly practiced getting her gestures and behavior right. To help hide the fact that she did not know how to read or write, they decided Ellen should wear her right arm in a sling. If she was a lame man, no one would expect her to sign her name to any registries. Because it was illegal to teach a slave to read and write, William was assumed to be illiterate, so no trace of our freedom-seeking couple could be found in any ship's log or hotel registry. Brilliant.

It was Christmastime when Ellen and William asked their respective "owners" if they could have a few days' leave. Luckily, because they were "favorite slaves," they were both granted time off and given passes to leave their respective homes for off-site visits. That gave them a few days' head start before anyone knew they had fled. They set out on their journey on December 21, 1848. Their escape took several days by train and by ship. Along the way they encountered slave owners who insisted to Ellen that "he" was treating his slave far too well. Ellen was scolded and told he shouldn't be traveling north with William, who was certain to try to escape. Ellen, as the infirm businessman, even garnered the attention of a young woman on one of the trains. Can you imagine? "*Not now, friend, I am in the middle of something!*"

Not much is known about how the Crafts planned their route, how they researched train schedules, or how they decided which ships to take. Their escape hit a few snags along the way, but they always triumphed. For instance, the trip north nearly ended before it began when, on the very first train, as William rode in a segregated car for Black passengers and Ellen rode in first class, an acquaintance of Ellen's enslavers got on board. Ellen thought for certain that this man had been sent to retrieve them, but when the man addressed Ellen with "How do you do, sir?" she relaxed and feigned deafness the rest of the journey. It must have been harrowing, the stress of the multiday escape and the exhaustion of the performances they both had to keep up at every minute. No disrespect to Mr. Craft, but make no mistake, the pressure rested most heavily on Ellen's shoulders, for it was Ellen who had to perform a different race, gender, and class. To be visible at a time when women, let alone African American women, were supposed to be very much invisible was an astonishing feat.

Although the Crafts had several close calls on their journey, they were successful in evading detection. They arrived in free Philadelphia early on the morning of Christmas Day. As they left the station, Ellen began to cry. They were free.

The underground abolitionist network immediately gave them assistance, including lodging and reading lessons. Three weeks later, they moved to Boston, where William began work as a cabinetmaker and Ellen soon found employment as a seamstress. However, their harrowing journey was not nearly over.

In 1850, the United States Congress passed the Fugitive Slave Act, which made it a federal crime to aid escaped slaves and permitted slave hunters to pursue escapees, even in free states. Their notoriety made the Crafts particularly vulnerable. Utilizing what was known as the "slave patrol system," the Crafts' former owners sent "slave catchers" to retrieve them, while abolitionist members of the newly formed Committee of Safety and Vigilance sought to safeguard the couple.

In December 1850, two years after making their daring escape, Ellen and William no longer felt safe in the North and fled to England. The hunters had been persistent, and despite the best efforts of an interracial coalition of allies in the North, the couple was in constant danger of capture. Not only did Ellen's former owner send bounty hunters up north to retrieve them, but that remarkable asshole even appealed to the president of the United States, Millard Fillmore, to intervene so he could regain his "property." The president agreed (the fuckery!) that the Crafts should be returned to their enslavers in the South and authorized the use of military force if necessary to take them. So, yeah, it was a good idea to leave. "It was not until we stepped upon the shore at Liverpool that we were free from every slavish fear," wrote the Crafts.

Ellen and William settled in Surrey and then West London, where they raised five children. They dedicated their lives to the abolitionist movement and women's rights, and their memoir was published on the eve of the Civil War. They returned to Georgia in 1870, and in 1873 the Crafts founded the Woodville Co-operative Farm School for the education and employment of freedmen.

One final note about Ellen Craft. In the era in which the Crafts lived, society adhered to strict gender roles. Despite this, Ellen is remembered for her activism as well as her ingenious escape. She accompanied her husband to antislavery meetings in the United States and in England and appeared regularly with him on public stages, though he would have been the more vocal of the two. As professor and author Barbara McCaskill put it, "This decision to cultivate a public presence visibly communicated that she was not willing to shrink into the shadows now that she was free." Ellen Craft was an iconoclast, a hero, a mother, a survivor. An absolute inspiration.

DOROTHY LAWRENCE

More than anything, Dorothy Lawrence wanted to be a journalist. After the outbreak of World War I, this dream swiftly morphed into "war correspondent," and when she was rejected by every newspaper and by the War Office, nineteen-year-old Dorothy set out to reach the Western Front all on her own. With no credentials and no news outlet backing her . . . she did it.

How far would you go to realize your dreams? I remember telling my parents when I was a teenager that I was going to be an actor and they were like, uhhhh that's cute, but you have to go to an Actual Real University with Actual Real Professors, *and*, they went on, instead of the *ridiculous* choice of acting, we think you should study journalism because that's a more stable career choice (AHAHAHAHA said every person who has been alive the past thirty years). But I am a very persuasive person, and I simply *told* Lise and Bob that I was GOING to theater school. We met in the middle, and I agreed to study theater at an accredited university. All this is to say, I thought I was a rather bold teenager. And then I discovered Dorothy Lawrence.

Dorothy was born in England to a single mom in 1896; exactly where seems to be up for debate. Almost all the literature on Dorothy tell slightly different stories about where she was born and to whom. If we rely on her own words, she referred to herself as an only child and an orphan, which lines up with what many historians recount about her mother dying when Dorothy was about thirteen or fourteen and Dorothy then being placed in a guardian's care.

During her early teens, the struggle for women's rights and the right to vote was heating up in the United Kingdom. The movement challenged age-old perceptions about the role of women. Journalism was still very much a man's game, but Dorothy was determined to break in. The pieces she would have been assigned as a young writer likely would have been limited to light topics and "women's issues." You know, like, "Shepherd's Pie: Cheese or No Cheese?" or "Is Wearing a Ribbon in My Hair Asking for It?" But Dorothy had her sights set on so much more. This ambitious young woman knew she would need a real scoop to get noticed.

When World War I broke out, my girl Dot had a crazy idea. She approached every newspaper in London, asking them to fund her getting to the front. They looked at her like she was mad, and, unsurprisingly, they all said no. Seasoned journalists, *real* journalists (read: *men*), were having an impossible time getting over there, *you think we're gonna send a girl?* But do you think that deterred her? You bet your sweet boobies it did not.

It turns out Dorothy wrote a book about her adventures getting to the Western Front: *Sapper Dorothy Lawrence: The Only English Woman Soldier, Late Royal Engineers, 51st Division 179th Tunnelling Company, B.E.F.* (1919).

With the very first words of the book, Dorothy tells us how she packed up her bicycle and in June 1915 traveled by ferry from Folkestone, England, to Boulogne, France, all by herself at the age of nineteen, to be closer to the front so she could potentially report on it—that alone, dear reader, that alone and I was already enchanted. Listen, I travel a lot by myself, but even in 2021 there are loads of people who can't fathom solo travel. (If you are reading this, every human adult, elder, or child, please go take a trip by yourself, it will change your life. Okay, maybe not child. Please don't hitchhike to Nashville and tell your mom I told you to.) Here comes teenage Dorothy in 1915, not on some jaunt to New York City to see a few Broadway shows, NO: hopping on a boat with her bike, headed to a foreign land—*a battle-ravaged country*—yearning to change her life and accomplish something truly unheard of. Wow.

After arriving by ferry, Dorothy spent weeks biking around northern France, living among soldiers on leave, talking to civilians, and I hope eating lots of pastry. She knew she needed to get closer to the front, and eventually realized she wouldn't be able to do that as a woman. In Paris she befriended a couple of soldiers, boys from back home, who agreed to smuggle her the makings of a khaki soldier's uniform. These blokes taught her military drills and walked with her in the streets of Paris, coaching her on how to move like a man. I mean, this is a movie, isn't it? Can't you see it? She convinced another soldier, a military policeman at the Gare Saint-Lazare, to cut off her hair while our two friendly Brits helped forge her a new identity and a travel pass. Although she wasn't exactly sure when it would best serve her to use the disguise, once she put it all together, along with several layers of bandages and padding to mask her curves, she would be able to transform herself into Private Denis Smith!

After getting some bad directions in Amiens, she landed in Albert (in the Somme) instead of her intended destination, Béthune. It was best that she continued to blend in with the locals, so Dorothy was still dressed as a lady (a lady with a very peculiar haircut) and her presence baffled the military men. Her pass was for Béthune, so they told her she had to leave, but just as she was about to depart, she stopped herself. You see, the town of Albert was known as "the front of the front." She was so close to the trenches! Albert was where she needed to be, and fate had brought her there.

I love that in her book Dorothy, like every good female comedian of days gone by, makes silly, self-deprecating, but not mean, cracks about her appearance, her looks, her body . . . she's a regular Phyllis Diller. (Real quick, if you're too young to know who Phyllis Diller was, please go look her up. My favorite of her one-liners, which I think Dorothy would have loved: "I was the world's ugliest baby. When I was born, the doctor slapped everybody.") Dorothy had trashed her corset and petticoat sometime after she left Paris, because when it came time to do the old switcheroo into Denis, she didn't want some random female undergarments lying around. She jokes in the book about not having her shaping garments to hold her together and about the "multitude of deficiencies" that were on display. Oh, sweet girl!

At this point Dorothy was fortunate enough to befriend diminutive, middle-aged soldier Sapper Tommy Dunn, who, Dot said, "championed my cause at the outset." Sappers were part of Royal Engineer tunneling companies, specialist units in the British Army that were formed to dig attack tunnels under enemy lines during World War I. During trench warfare, sappers, who were often experienced civilian miners who had been rejected for combat duty due to age or ill health (see wee aging Tom Dunn), would complete a mine and then fill it with explosives, sometimes hundreds of tons, and then detonate them. They followed with an attack on the surprised survivors from the destroyed position. Dorothy was about to become Sapper Denis Smith.

Fun fact: Months after Dorothy left France, her tunneling company, the 179th, played an important role on the first day of the infamous Battle of the Somme, when it was responsible for detonating the Lochnagar mine at 7:28 a.m. on July 1, 1916. The mine's explosion obliterated three or four hundred feet of German dugouts, all thought to have been full of German troops. The crater left behind is three hundred feet wide and is one of the most visited spots on what was the Western Front. More than one million soldiers perished during the Battle of the Somme, one of the bloodiest battles in human history. Okay, maybe it's not a *fun* fact.

After taking up residence in a half-blasted-out cottage near the company's barracks, Dorothy spent several days and nights waiting, practicing, and intermittently starving. Finally, one night Tommy Dunn arrived to say that they were marching out that evening, and, if she wanted, Dorothy-as-Denis could easily blend in with the rest of the men, marching to the front under the cover of night. She began her transformation: "Enveloping myself in swathes of bandages, like a mummy, I pulled these swathes taut around my body . . . even then the waistline showed above the dip of my back. So I padded my back with layers of cotton wool."

According to Rebecca Nash, curator of the Royal Engineers Museum, "The sappers' uniform would have given Dorothy some leeway to move around—tunnellers had a kind of right to roam. They were not subject to the same military strictures as infantry soldiers, for example, and would often turn up without the commanding officer of an infantry regiment having been informed. It was the perfect cover."

So, yes, dear reader, Dorothy made it to the front! She dug trenches and she filled mines with explosives alongside her buddy Tom Dunn. After some time in the trenches, Dorothy tells us, "Fainting fits started to bring disgrace on the King's uniform after ten days and nights spent under almost incessant fire." She felt so unwell that she feared she could easily be found out or captured and was worried she was putting her comrades at risk. She decided to take a sergeant into her confidence and came clean about who she was. His response

SAPPER DOROTHY LAWRENCE

was along the lines of "…Okay," which relieved our girl immensely. But only a few hours later a couple of officers showed up to arrest her! Dot snarled at the sergeant who betrayed her, telling him he was lucky she wasn't a man because she would've knocked him on his ass right there. She was PISSED.

After she was detained, Dorothy was bounced around to different locations, each time being put through a new series of cross-examinations and interrogations: colonels, army headquarters officers, secret intelligence officers, everyone wanted an opportunity to grill her. She was officially deemed a prisoner of war. Some were delighted to be in the company of such a bold young lady. Others were disgusted by what this "little girl" had done. One came right out and sneered, "*Why don't you marry?*" Most of them were completely baffled by her and didn't know whether she was a spy or a "camp follower" (a super chill way of saying "prostitute"). "We don't know what you are," one of them said right to her face, even as she repeatedly told them about her designs on getting to the front so she could report on it. The question I have is, Was female ambition so baffling? Was the very concept of a woman endeavoring to be a war correspondent, determined to achieve her goal by the most extreme measures . . . was that *so* hard to grasp? Yes, reader, apparently it was.

At one point she told all the distinguished officers staring her down, needling her with questions, that they should be listening to her and be grateful to her for all that she was telling them. Because a German girl, an *actual* spy, could easily achieve what she did, *and*, she told them, you should really be looking at *yourselves* and how you all could improve because of what I was able to do here. She was like, Look, I know I crossed a line, but *I was able to* and that's on you. YOU SHOULD BE THANKING ME. I mean, obviously I'm paraphrasing, but you get it, she was splendid.

Now, you probably think these lads couldn't wait to get rid of our fine mouthy gal and ship her back to jolly old England. Not so fast. They wanted to keep her where they could see her at least until after the big Battle of Loos, just in case she had information she could use against them. So where did they put her? Why, the nearby Convent de Bon Pasteur, which housed an order of cloistered nuns. Cloistered, meaning these sisters *never* left. Well, the nuns adored her. They couldn't believe what she had accomplished and were teeming with questions. Again, I'm sorry, but don't you want to see this movie?!

The powers that be finally released Dorothy and sent her home to England. She was overcome with mixed feelings as she stepped on the boat at Boulogne. How she wished she were a roving war correspondent instead of a girl being sent home with a slapped wrist. Not only did she not attain any actual scoops to give to the English papers, but she was also forbidden to write a single word about her experiences until after the armistice in 1918.

Dorothy's book was released in 1919 to mixed reviews, and while it initially did well, it was remaindered within a year. A review in the *Spectator* mocked her efforts, calling her "a girlish freak." Many people spun her story to be an utter failure, which, for my money, couldn't be further from the truth, and, frankly, I'm offended!

By the mid-1920s, the book had been all but forgotten and Dorothy's mental health had deteriorated. She accused one of her guardians of rape. While there are a lot of missing pieces to her story, it is well documented that she spent from 1925 until her death in 1964 in hospitals—first in the Hanwell Asylum, and from 1952 in Friern Mental Hospital. An absolute heartbreaker. According to the historian Simon Jones, who is currently researching and writing a book on Lawrence:

> *At the time she was committed her account of the rape was seen as delusional, manic behaviour, but if it was true it might go some way to explaining why she did what she did during the 1st World War. We know today that victims of sexual abuse do not value their own well-being—did Dorothy deliberately put herself in danger by going to France? If she understood the danger she was in, she did not seem to fear it. Albert in the Somme in those days was somewhere even the soldiers tried to avoid—they would even deliberately injure themselves—yet she headed straight for it.*

Again, this sounds a bit like a man trying to make sense of fiery, female ambition: she must have been traumatized to do what she did. Of course, we will never know all that was in Dorothy's heart, but I would like to think that, even by putting herself in harm's way, she was in fact trying to *save* herself. If she had a heavy, traumatized heart, if she was a rape survivor who lost her mom at the precious age of thirteen or fourteen, was she not trying to truly LIVE by doing what she did? She clearly had moxie and a talent for telling stories. She took extreme measures to try to make a name for herself as a writer. To stake her claim. To become something *more* than illegitimate daughter, orphan, or rape survivor. To become fully herself and to commit completely to her dreams. Her dreams were never fully realized, it's true. I wish they had been. She was funny. She was brave. She was a fighter. And while I wish millions had read her book and knew her name, it is that moment young Dorothy stepped onto the ferry in Folkestone that makes her an absolute success in my eyes.

Dorothy's incredible story was dismissed as folklore for more than eighty years, until Richard Bennett, the grandson of Richard Samson Bennett, one of the soldiers who aided Dorothy in her adventure, found mention of her while researching his family history at the Royal Engineers Museum, and Simon Jones unearthed a copy of her autobiography. A copy of said book has been scanned and is available to read online. I highly recommend it.

I will leave the last word to Dorothy:

No one realizes better than myself that in writing this true account without shelter of nom de plume, I am incurring the risk of personal reputation. Knowing the risk I run, I accept its consequences. I write this book as a tribute; rather in the light of discharging a debt do I set out this true story and write under my own name. Many readers will readily discredit this tale; and discredit rests on two distinct charges—facts queried and personal character assailed. To "take cover" under the cowardly shelter of a nom de plume, I do not feel inclined. Anyway I offer at least Fair-play by revealing as target my true identity. I come out into the open.

HATSHEPSUT

A ncient Egypt achieved the peak of its power during the Eighteenth Dynasty, also known as the Thutmosid Dynasty (ca. 1550–1295 BCE). Hatshepsut was the fifth pharaoh of the Eighteenth Dynasty, and while other women had reigned in Egypt before, Hatshepsut was the first female to rule long term. When we combine her regency and her kingship, she reigned for more than twenty years, and according to Egyptologists and ancient texts alike, she was one of the most successful pharaohs ever.

So why have so few of us heard of her? Is it because there was no bloodshed, no coup, no major drama that we know of? Maybe it's because she was a *successful* woman leader, and those stories are never very compelling, certainly not as entertaining and patriarchy validating as the tales

of female leaders whose legacies include seduction, murder, and military disasters. Those tales seem to have little trouble enduring throughout history, helping enforce the horseshit notion that women can't be trusted and should never rule.

Hatshepsut was a woman who did everything right, and then her successors tried to wipe her and her magnificence from history. To add insult to injury, early Egyptologists and scholars went on to try to shame and discredit her, painting her as a woman who took something that was never hers for the taking: power. These chaps (yeah, #notallmen but in this case 100 percent all men) tried their best to rewrite Hatshepsut's remarkable, long, prosperous, and peaceful reign as a tale of deceit and revenge. Sigh.

But let's start at the beginning.

While it was not customary for ancient Egyptian girls to be educated, Hatshepsut was no ordinary girl. She was the most high born offspring of the Thutmosid family, her father being King Thutmose I and her mother being Queen Ahmose, the "King's Great Wife" (the most highly ranked wife *and* the most important "vessel" for his off to spring from). You gotta love the "King's Great Wife." What comes next? The "King's Meh Wife," followed by the dreaded bottom rung, "King's Shit Wife"?

Because of her lineage, Hatshepsut received formal education, and from birth it was understood that she would marry the next king, who, wouldn't you know, was going to be one of her brothers. But, as fate would have it, both of her brothers died, and when her father also ascended to the sky, plan B had to be enacted: Thutmose II would have to be a son born from one of her dad's secondary wives, and by marrying the fully royal Hatshepsut, his status would be elevated. Hatshepsut would legitimize her half brother enough for him to be king. There's patriarchy for ya. She could legitimize him to be ruler of the land, but she herself could not rule. At least not yet.

By the way, Hatshepsut was about twelve years old at this point.

In addition to Hatshepsut becoming the new "King's Great Wife," her father had also designated her as the first in the Thutmosid Dynasty to be "God's Wife of Amun"—a huge deal. After she married the king, she was both "God's Wife" and the "King's Great Wife," meaning she held the two most important posts an ancient Egyptian female could hold, surpassing even her own mother's status.

As "God's Wife," preteen Hatshepsut possessed her own estates and palaces and had a team of people handling her affairs. She also routinely practiced a ritual of conception with the god Amun, whom Egyptologist Kara Cooney describes as a solid gold statue "crafted with an erect penis full of potentiality and creation." Cooney elaborates that Egyptian texts clearly state how Amun "enacted his self-re-creation through an act of masturbation" with the God's Wife, who provided "the 'activity' that a statue of a god was unable to provide for himself." Hatshepsut facilitated the ongoing creation of the universe by holding the statue's penis so Amun could orgasm, which in turn caused him to be reborn, and according to ancient Egyptians, this most sacred act literally made the world go round. In Cooney's words, when she helped the god get himself off, "Hatshepsut was to assist the very machinery of the cosmos." Tight.

From the start, Hatshepsut's hubby, King Thutmose II, was a sickly fellow—not uncommon for the era. Cholera, smallpox, malaria, various parasites—literally so many worms, you guys. It didn't matter if you were lowborn or highborn, everyone was sick or in pain at all times in the ancient world. As was customary, the new king was spreading his seed all over Thebes, trying to make a son with Hatshepsut (that ideal vessel!) and with perhaps dozens of "beauties" and lesser wives in his harem. By the time her ailing husband died, likely still in his twenties, Hatshepsut had given birth to a girl, Nefrure, but no boys. A son born from one of the harem wives, still a baby or a toddler at that point, was once again chosen to be the next king, Thutmose III.

Hatshepsut first began to lead when she stepped in as this new baby king's regent, a common practice. According to Cooney's *The Woman Who Would Be King* (2014), "The office of queen-regent was ancient by the time Hatshepsut exercised it. Evidence for the practice of highborn, educated women ruling on behalf of their young male charges goes back to the Old Kingdom at least, almost one thousand years before."

Hatshepsut took to leadership exceedingly well. She was smart, she was pious, she could hold her own with anyone. Maybe it was her great lineage. Maybe it was all those years helping Amun re-create the universe.

Like her father, Hatshepsut launched an excellent building program. Cooney surmises, "The documentation of her building activity . . . during her regency indicates a level of construction, job creation, and income for priests and temple bureaucrats that had never been seen before in Egypt." Hatshepsut had witnessed the impact of her father's ambitious building projects, learning that they could simultaneously be job creators, propaganda machines, *and* gifts to the gods . . . so much bang for your pharaoh buck!

There is some debate, but most scholars agree that it was about year seven of Thutmose III's reign (but really, Hatshepsut's reign . . . remember, T3 is still a little kid) that the impossible occurred: Hatshepsut herself was crowned king—well, more like co-king. The kid was never pushed out of the picture, but he was definitely the junior king. Hatshepsut clearly had become very popular, and by all accounts everyone seemed to support and even assist her ascension. She was building, she was reestablishing trade routes, she was amassing wealth, and people were into it! Everything she did was also steeped in religious piety, as directed by Amun. An inscription on Hatshepsut's obelisk at Karnak reads, "I acted under his command; it was he who led me. I did not plan a work without his doing. It was he who gave directions." She was like, "Guys, Amun *told* me I was king. What am I gonna do, *argue with Amun*??"

So, this is where the sexism comes in. Old-timey historian types and early Egyptologists once painted Hatshepsut as a vile usurper, her rise to power evidence of naked, conniving ambition, because of course they did. Sigh. William C. Hayes, curator of Egyptian art at the Metropolitan Museum, wrote in 1953, "It was not long before this vain, ambitious, and unscrupulous woman showed herself in her true colors." Billy, honey, be careful, your misogyny is showing.

Renée Dreyfus, curator of ancient art and interpretation at the Fine Arts Museums of San Francisco, nails it in a 2006 article in *Smithsonian Magazine*. "So much of what was written about Hatshepsut, I think, had to

do with who the archaeologists were . . . gentlemen scholars of a certain generation." And, I'll add, ones who clearly had mommy issues.

More recent scholarship—i.e., expertise not clouded by an Oedipal complex—suggests that a political crisis such as a threat from a competing branch of the royal family may have compelled Hatshepsut to become pharaoh. Far from stealing the throne, says Catharine Roehrig, former curator of Egyptian art at the Metropolitan Museum, "Hatshepsut may have had to declare herself king to protect the kingship for her stepson." And remember, the kid king was only eight or nine years old at that point and no one even knew if he was going to survive childhood (see worms and pestilence above). Hatshepsut *did what she had to do*.

In the early years of her kingship, Hatshepsut is portrayed wearing the traditional garb of a woman and the crown of the king, which was bold and unique. At some point, as little Thutmose III grew older, she seemed to understand that something different needed to be communicated by her image. Statues and other royal imagery began depicting her as more masculine, with broad shoulders, strong pec muscles, and no breasts. Eventually she went all in, and depictions of her became deeply masculinized in face and in body, including a beard. Scholars consider the possibility that she even sometimes bound her breasts and wore the traditional male garb and fake beard during temple rituals. This process was gradual and seems directly related to her retaining power and status as king, projecting an image that said, "I've got you. I'm your king. Look at my beard."

When Thutmose III got older, he could have taken steps to have Hatshepsut removed, but he didn't. It appears there was no animosity between them. It was only later, after Hatshepsut had died and T3 was nearing the end of his own reign, that he attempted to have evidence of her scrubbed and had her name removed from the list of kings. *Ouch.* Experts say it was likely not an act of vengeance but rather more about purifying the lineage from Thutmose I to himself without that distracting little TWENTY-YEAR female hiccup in there, breaking the line. Egyptologist Peter Dorman posits that Hatshepsut's reign may have been *too* successful, a dangerous precedent "best erased, to prevent the possibility of another powerful female ever inserting herself into the long line of Egyptian male kings." *It's not personal, it's patriarchy.* No one knows how Hatshepsut died, but after ruling from about 1479 to 1458 BCE, the woman who began as a "King's Daughter" and went on to become the greatest female leader Egypt would ever know was dead.

Among her many ambitious building projects, her greatest achievement was her enormous memorial temple at Deir el-Bahri, considered one of the region's architectural wonders. During her reign she expanded the trade routes of ancient Egypt, most notably her expedition to Punt, where no Egyptian had been for five hundred years. This remarkable undertaking resulted in gold, ivory, exotic animals, and live myrrh trees, signifying the first known successful attempt at transplanting foreign fauna. Hatshepsut constructed on a grander scale than any pharaoh before her or, with the exception of Ramesses II (1279–1213 BCE), any who came after.

There is evidence that suggests Hatshepsut tried to elevate her daughter, Nefrure, to be her female heir so that Nefrure could continue in some sort of female co-kingship after her, but with no success. I love that she was the first long-reigning female pharaoh and that she attempted to continue this concept of female rule with her own daughter, trying to change the way the system had always been. It didn't work, but wow— so bloody cool that she tried.

In the beginning, when she became regent, she was most likely inspired to save her family's dynasty, but along the way I think Hatshepsut's own excellence and achievements made her realize her abilities and made her believe that patriarchal rule should and could be updated. I wish I could tell her we are still trying in the twenty-first century.

CHRISTIAN CADDELL, WITCH-PRICKER

E very woman in this book may be a badass, but not every woman in this book is a hero. In Europe during the sixteenth and seventeenth centuries there was widespread panic about malevolent Satanic witches operating as an organized threat to Christianity. The ongoing inquisitions, which spanned three centuries, saw massive witch hunts, including trials, tortures, and executions at which an estimated forty thousand to one hundred thousand people were killed. It might be unnecessary to point out, but witches were almost always discovered to be women.

Between 1661 and 1662, the number of witch trials and executions reached record levels in post-Reformation Scotland, where the number of executions per capita was five times the European average—the majority of which, again, were women. For a country that small, this statistic is striking and rather horrific. While there are memorials throughout Scotland, in 2019, about three hundred years after the last execution of a woman accused of witchcraft, calls began growing for a national memorial to the thousands who were tortured and killed.

During the height of the witch trials, several methods were used to "prove" that a person was a witch. There was the fun sink-or-swim test, which posited that an innocent/non-witch would sink to the bottom of a body of water, while a dirty evil witch would simply bob up and down at the surface. So, you know, floating. GREAT SYSTEM, GUYS. TOTALLY NOT RIGGED. Perhaps the most chilling method for identifying a witch, however, was the practice of witch-pricking. Yeah, I hadn't heard of it either.

Professional witch-prickers earned a handsome living by unmasking witches, traveling from town to town to perform their ghastly services. The pricker's job was to test for "the devil's mark," a spot where a pin or a needle could be plunged into the body without causing bleeding or pain. A word of advice: When you start getting depressed about still having to fight for some of our rights and freedoms, one thing you could do is remember how much worse it used to be. Remind yourself that olden times were innnnnnnnnsane, especially for women. Witch-prickers are the stuff of horror films: a man—yes, always a man—in a tall hat and the dark cloak of a Puritan who rolls into town to terrorize its citizens. Witch-pricking: nice work if you can get it, but ya gotta be a dude!

But what if the witch-pricker was a woman in disguise?

In Scotland in 1662, that's exactly what happened. A woman named Christian Caddell had watched one of Scotland's most famous witch-prickers at work (you know, the totally normal public display of a woman having her head shaved and then being forced to strip so that long pins and needles could be plunged into her body) and thought to herself, "I could do that!" She went on to reinvent herself as John Dickson, Witch-Pricker. It's sort of like when you see someone successfully doing stand-up comedy, there's a certain type of person in the audience who thinks, "Pfft! I could do that, that looks easy!" Wait, scratch that, it's nothing like that. Okay, maybe it's a little like that.

So, this opportunistic lady (and let's be honest, likely terrified, given the times) sees this bloke with his all-black getup, his tall hat, and his low-rent set of horror tools, and she surmises, "This is all a creepy pantomime, so why can't I don the costume and make a pretty penny, too?" Is there a special place in hell for a woman who seeks to earn her fortune this way? Talk about women not supporting other women. Yikes.

As terrible as Christian sounds, there's also a survival element to this story that I can't help but ponder. You see, nobody scrutinized a witch-pricker too closely for fear of capturing their attention. No one wanted to be on the receiving end of their . . . probe. So, by disguising herself as a man AND a witch-pricker, Caddell was not only bringing in some dough, but she was also eliminating herself from scrutiny—or at least one would hope. Maybe we can't entirely blame a potentially terrified gal for trying to save her hide any way she could. Times were pretty damn tough back then! But no question, she doesn't get a total pass . . . witch-pricking was evil. And to make matters even worse, the pricks (see what I did there) were paid extra for every witch they could positively identify. I think we can all agree that is a shit system, crafted and created to punish, hurt, and kill women. Thumbs all the way down.

In the end, the tables turned on "John Dickson" when he pointed his pricker at the wrong person. The story goes that Dickson accused a man named John Hay, who happened to be an influential court messenger, and was subsequently arrested. Maybe ya shoulda stuck with accusing women, huh? Did you get *cocky*? "Dickson" was not only arrested but he himself was then accused of witchcraft (game meet game) and interrogated in Edinburgh in August 1662 on the basis of "false accusation, torture, and causing death of innocent people in Moray." I mean, that should have been the charge brought against every single witch hunter ever! Shockingly, Caddell was not sentenced to death for her transgressions but was instead deported to a fever-ridden plantation in Barbados and never heard from again. But let the record show that dressing up as a man, pretending to be a witch-pricker, and condemning innocent people to death was considered a lesser offense than being a witch—an entirely made-up thing.

While it was a truly horrific time in history, the whole thing is also a bit of a joke. Hundreds of years of making-the-rules-up-as-you-go nonsense. You're a witch! No, YOU'RE a witch! The pious patriarchy acted out a sick and twisted dumb show, resulting in thousands upon thousands of dead and tortured innocent people. Christian Caddell dressed up as a witch-pricker and falsely accused people of being witches, which is exactly what her male colleagues were doing. A horror comedy.

MARGARET KING

M argaret King was born into extraordinary privilege and means. All that her family expected of her was to look comely, marry well, and pop out some babies. Margaret, however, had other plans, and the seeds of her radicalism were planted when her parents accidentally hired an ardent feminist writer and thinker to be her governess.

In 1786, when Mary Wollstonecraft was twenty-seven years old, before she had written her seminal work, *A Vindication of the Rights of Woman* (1792), she needed money. So, in the great tradition of writers and thinkers needing to supplement their income by serving others, and with no small resentment, she took a job as a governess in Ireland, minding some of the most privileged children in the land, in a damn castle no less—Mitchelstown Castle in County Cork. She joined an eighty-person staff and attended to the three daughters of Caroline and Robert King, Lord and Lady Kingsborough.

One might assume that the parents who hired Mary as governess knew that she'd written a book called *Thoughts on the Education of Daughters* (1787) and that was one of the reasons they hired her, but, believe it or not, nope. Wollstonecraft's *Thoughts* was critical of everything the Kings believed in as far as child-rearing went. Not only is the book adamantly pro-breastfeeding—a hotly contested practice in the eighteenth century—but it is also blatantly critical of the all-too-common way girls were educated: training that included acting fake and playing cards. *Thoughts* advocates for an education based on early childhood reading, benevolence, and love—quite literally the opposite of how the castle-bound, silver-spooned King kids were being raised when Wollstonecraft showed up. The more one discovers about the Kings, it doesn't come as a shock that they were in the dark about who they had hired to mind their daughters. It seems they were very proficient at making babies (twelve in total) but less adept at raising, loving, or spending any time with them. That's what the "hirelings" were for.

Mary's arrival at Mitchelstown had a massive impact on all the daughters, but on one perhaps more than the rest. Margaret King was the eldest daughter, likely born about 1772 or 1773 to teenage heiress Caroline, who was about seventeen at the time. Caroline was almost continuously pregnant, given her ongoing utilization of wet nurses to suckle her babies. Mary's *Vindication* contains several anecdotes and characterizations clearly gleaned from her time with the Kings, including what appear to be scathing portrayals of Caroline as the "fine lady" who was "reckoned very handsome, by those who do not miss the mind when the face is plump and fair" (*omg burn, Mary*) and as the woman who "took her lapdog to her bosom instead of her child."

Caroline doting on her dogs instead of her children was certainly not anomalous. As Margaret put it, people in their "rank of life" were "too much occupied by frivolous amusements to pay much attention to their offspring," which just makes me sad. As someone who is never going to have offspring, I can't help but think of all the fun shit Caroline and Robert missed out on, like teaching a toddler-sized person who looks just like you to say, "Piss off!"

For much of their childhood, Margaret and her siblings were shuttled from one grand family home to another and cared for almost exclusively by hired help. It was in this desert of parental neglect that the hydrating presence of Mary appeared. Mary's teachings and unorthodox beliefs, paired with affection and attention, held complete sway over Margaret and changed her forever. Mary railing against income inequality and speaking plainly about women's rights taught Margaret things she might never have learned otherwise. If it were any other governess, the girls would have been taught needlepoint and how to be wifely, whereas Mary encouraged them to read novels, even though their mother did not approve. Lady Caroline is traipsing across Europe and not hugging her kids and she's like, "OH, AND ALSO DON'T READ." You don't get to tell me what to do, Aristocrat Teen Mom!

Before long, Caroline started to believe her girls were being radicalized by Mary. I mean, where is the lie? In her eyes Mary was ruining her daughters and their prospects for marriage. Margaret repeatedly rebelled against her mother's wishes and ultimately declared herself a devoted disciple of Wollstonecraft, which didn't help matters. Mary had shown up with a chip on her shoulder and had continually clashed with her bosses . . . it would, of course, all come to a head. Less than a year after she arrived at Mitchelstown, Mary was dismissed. Margaret would never see her again. What we see in Margaret's story, however, is that absence not only makes the heart grow fonder, but it also makes the influence grow stronger.

Rebel and Wollstonecraft disciple though she was, Margaret bent to her family's will when she married the highly suitable suitor Stephen Moore, 2nd Earl of Mount Cashell, making her Lady Mount Cashell. The marriage was likely more of a business transaction between two families than a love connection, and one that Margaret would come to regret. In a short autobiography she wrote for her children years later, Margaret admits, "I was therefore guilty of numerous errors and none greater than that of marrying at 19 a man whose character was perfectly opposite to mine." She continues:

> *Stephen Moore Earl of Mount Cashell was about one and twenty, a handsome man with gentle manners & the appearance of an easy temper. His education had been of the meanest sort; his understanding was uncultivated & his mind contracted. He had an aversion to literature, was incapable of comprehending the feelings of a noble spirit & respected nothing but wealth & titles—how he came to think of me for a wife God alone knows. To my shame I confess that I married him with the idea of governing him, the silliest project that ever entered a woman's mind.*

Who among us isn't guilty of trying to educate and mold a lover into being someone we actually want to hang with? It's one of those things you eventually learn NOT to do when you finally start to grow up. I don't mean the fake growing up of your twenties when you're basically still a child. I mean the *real* "Oh wait. Shit" growing up of your thirties. If you are reading this and still trying to change someone: STOP.

Despite her tepid feelings, Margaret wound up having eight children with Moore, which is a lot, but thems were the times. Then, while they were traveling in Europe and Margaret was pregnant with her eighth child, she met and fell in love with fellow Irishman George Tighe. For the first time in her life, she became aware of what desire and love felt like.

The decision to leave her husband was not a rash one—on the contrary. The child who was in utero when she met George was two years old when the Moore clan began their journey home to Ireland, and Margaret realized she could not return with them. (Aristocrats didn't travel abroad

for two or three weeks, y'all. These people vacationed for YEARS.) Things had gotten downright bad between Margaret and Stephen, and returning to Ireland, staying with him, meant more suffering than she was willing to withstand. She remained in Europe with the toddler, choosing love and Tighe. To have the courage to defy society in this way and pursue her own happiness would have been truly shocking. It meant completely relinquishing her rights to her children, as that was the law. It also meant losing all her money, her title, and status. The whole ordeal must have been gut wrenching. As an aside, when her husband demanded she give up her last child, the toddler Elizabeth, Margaret pressed her lawyer, shouldn't a mother have the right to keep a child under the age of seven? The answer was NO—such a right would not become law until 1839. Oof.

Margaret described her husband as "a very weak man" whose friends had convinced him "that his character would rise on the ruins of mine. Whether he really intends to shut my own doors against me & separate me from my children I know not, but nothing shall prevent me from endeavouring to be of use to them for whose sake I have endured more than anyone has notion of, in the way of petty tyranny and trifling opposition." Although she's quoted as saying something to the effect of "over my dead body," Margaret was forced to make the painful journey back to Ireland in 1807 to hand over Elizabeth.

Margaret was heartbroken, but her newfound freedom—and perhaps the jolt that comes from being in love—led her to pursue a dream that was unfathomable, not to mention illegal, for most women at the time. Inspired once again by Mary Wollstonecraft, who believed that women should "study the art of healing, and be physicians as well as nurses," Margaret decided to study medicine in Jena, Germany, and she did so disguised as a man. Bolstered by Wollstonecraft's teachings, Margaret also believed she had a natural inclination in this area, having already raised six children with strong constitutions, something she attributed to the breastfeeding and care she offered them in their early years. We must remember that a LOT of children died in those days. She was proud of her achievement: healthy, living children. To Margaret and Mary, women and mothers made natural caregivers, so why not physicians? If she had to dress as a man to receive the training, so be it.

She and George eventually moved to Italy, where Margaret continued her medical studies with Andrea Vaccà Berlinghieri, a renowned professor of surgery who was also a freethinking liberal (i.e., he respected Margaret as an equal despite her vagina). Under his guidance Margaret ran a medical practice and an infirmary for the poor. Long before doctors concerned themselves with even mere cleanliness, Margaret promoted preventative and alternative medicine, advising against unnecessary drugs and treatments. Some say Margaret invented a gentle form of pediatrics long before pediatrics was even an established branch of medicine. The evidence can be found in her book *Advice to Young Mothers on the Physical Education of Children* (1823).

After leaving her husband, Margaret lost the title of Lady Mount Cashell and legally couldn't be Mrs. Tighe, so, after a lifetime of others choosing for her, it came time for her to choose her own name. She decided to be known as Mrs. Mason, proving that Mary Wollstonecraft's influence was still alive and kicking. Mary's experiences during the year she spent with the Kings not only made their way into her philosophical writings, but they also turned up in her only children's book, *Original Stories from Real Life* (1788). The girl in the book is based on Margaret, and the maternal teacher who frames the stories is named Mrs. Mason. The girl dreams aloud at one point, "I wish to be a woman and to be like Mrs. Mason." Margaret grew up and she became Mrs. Mason. What poetry and devotion. What a beautiful mark Mary left on her pupil.

In Italy, Mrs. Mason grew more and more into her own. She birthed a literary society called Accademia dei Lunatici, or Academy of Lunatics, attended by poets and future revolutionaries. "It cannot entirely be a coincidence that many of the forty-six members later played important roles in the history of the Italian Risorgimento," wrote Margaret's biographer, Edward C. McAleer, "and one is tempted to trace the liberalism of Mary Wollstonecraft into Italy by way of Mrs. Mason."

In a perfect chef's-kiss full-circle moment, more than thirty years after Mary had nurtured young Margaret, Margaret did the same for Wollstonecraft's daughter, author Mary Shelley, and her poet husband, Percy. She helped and advised them, assisted them in relocating to Italy. She was a maternal sort of figure to Mary's daughter, who never knew her mother, who had died tragically of septicemia days after giving birth.

Margaret's *Advice to Young Mothers* was published in the United States, Britain, and Italy, and remains in print today. In addition to preventative medical advice for children, it also advises on the evils of corsetry, the superiority of female midwives over male physicians, and the benefits of breastfeeding. It has Mary's influence and inspiration all over it, not the least of which is its mere existence. After Mary was discharged from her governess position with the Kings, she wrote to her sister, newly determined to be a professional writer who lived entirely off her writing—no small ambition. At the time, it was not uncommon for works published by women writers to include a preface in which the author *apologized* for the transgressive immodesty of being published, explaining a financial need. Wow. And then there's Mary Wollstonecraft, who wrote to her sister, "I am then going to be the first of a new genus—I tremble at the attempt." This new genus: a woman who writes and publishes UNAPOLOGETICALLY. Mary Wollstonecraft was the living, breathing proof that female authorship could be a thing . . . if you can see it, you can be it. Margaret was one who saw it and then became it.

One frequently imagines a soul mate as someone you are meant to be with, a lover, a spouse. When I read about Margaret and Mary, I imagine *them* as soul mates. It makes me tear up to think of the lasting imprint Mary made on young Margaret in one solitary year. That imprint then became a series of small waves, rippling out, living on and on, affecting countless others as Margaret eventually made the bold decision to live her own life exactly as she pleased, carrying the Wollstonecraft torch everywhere she went.

Margaret, who died in her early sixties in 1835, had many monikers in her lifetime. She began life as Margaret King then became Margaret Moore, or Lady Mount Cashell, and finally Mrs. Mason. The one moniker we don't know is the male pseudonym Margaret adopted when she attended medical school. I wish I knew it. Maybe I'd ask my friends to start referring to me as such. I'd love to carry the torch.

MARY

MARGARET

MARY II

63

MARIA TOORPAKAI

Maria Toorpakai is a professional squash player who, as a child, dressed as a boy to play and compete in sports, defying the Taliban. She is also a Grade-A, Certified Boss. Maria was born November 22, 1990, in South Waziristan, FATA (Federally Administered Tribal Areas). This semi-autonomous tribal region in northwestern Pakistan is considered one of the most dangerous places on earth, known for breeding terrorists and super duper not known for advancing the rights of women. Although she was born to enlightened, loving, open-minded parents, Toorpakai lived in a place where girls were not allowed to leave the house without a male companion, let alone run and play outside like little boys.

Maria was fortunate because her father was a forward thinker who believed in education and in equality. Her mom was part of a tiny percentage of Wazir women whose parents had encouraged education. On the night her parents married—the night they met—Maria's dad gave her mom a Levi's jean jacket "from America." They spent the rest of that first night standing in front of a full-length mirror, both dressed in denim . . . and laughing. Her mother had been so afraid of who this stranger/husband would be, but after that night—and when he completely encouraged her continued education—her mother decided, "It was a miracle." These two, who make me cry every time because DENIM DRESS-UP WEDDING NIGHT, these *two* miracles were who made feisty, determined, hella strong Maria.

In Toorpakai's part of the world, a girl going outside alone and uncovered was forbidden, considered a sin against God—but that did not stop young Maria. She always longed to be out, running free like the boys she watched from her window. One day, when she was very little, she ventured outside. She discovered a group of men playing volleyball. She watched in awe as they smacked the ball and made it fly. She was enthralled.

At one point, a rogue ball flew toward her. Not being able to help herself and still being too young to fully know her place as a girl, she picked up the volleyball and smacked it back to the men. Maria recognized one of the men as the mullah from their mosque. At barely four years old, Maria didn't think she was doing anything wrong when she grinned at the men and said that she would like to play. Every one of their faces grew dark.

The mullah reached down and took ahold of her face, gripping her cheeks hard. In her memoir, *A Different Kind of Daughter* (2016), Maria wrote, "The slap to my face came so hard and fast that it sounded like a gunshot." He hit her two more times, keeping a hand gripped on her shoulder to keep her four-year-old body from falling backward.

Things started to become very clear to young Maria: "There was no in-between for girls like me who wanted to run outside and play games and sports in the open air. Suddenly, I was aware that, despite all of my liberal father's efforts . . . I would never truly be free. In our culture girls remained indoors, quiet and veiled for life."

Not long after, our young rebel went and gathered each and every one of her dresses, even the fanciest ones. She piled them in their cooking pit outside, dragged over the kerosene can with her strong little body, doused the dresses completely, and burned them to smithereens. She then ran into her house, found one of her brother's shalwar kameez, and put it on. She proceeded to the kitchen, got a sharp knife, and began hacking away at her hair, tossing it onto the burning dresses. She didn't know it, but her father was watching her, seeing his own sister in his headstrong, determined daughter, and he knew the truth: "A tomboy simply could not survive in the cage our culture expected girls to live in." He ran his fingers through Maria's butchered hair, laughing. In that moment he agreed that she could now live as his son, and he gifted his child a new name: Genghis Khan—i.e., *the greatest conqueror the world has ever known.* Have I mentioned how much I love Maria's father?

Maria's family moved several times during the years that followed, eventually settling in Peshawar, Pakistan, the first real city she ever laid eyes on. She was about ten and still living as Genghis Khan. About this time her father showed her what would become her favorite movie, the story of an underdog just like herself: *Rocky.* "Genghis" was always getting into fights. The brawling with hooligans in the streets escalated so much that Maria's father was determined to find a way for his child to channel all that energy elsewhere. Boxing wasn't a thing where they lived, so he took her to a gym and introduced her to weight lifting. She excelled at the sport but soon grew bored. One day, however, she drifted inside the gym next door and within seconds was transfixed by what would become her one true love: squash. Squash is huge in Pakistan.

At first only the coach knew Toorpakai's true female identity. Everyone on the team perceived her to be a boy. It helped that she was the biggest kid there. But one day the secret got out and suddenly the boys who had once admired her big, muscled arms were now belittling and mocking her. They called her a slut.

None of this deterred Maria. It motivated her. She was no longer hiding behind Genghis Khan. She was proud Wazir girl Maria Toorpakai. Her affinity for squash soon became an obsession. She had to be the best. She had to show them. How many of us women who have dared to tread in male-dominated spaces have felt like that? Raise your hand. Whoa, I just felt the breeze of a gazillion hands going up.

Maria did not have other girls to train with in Peshawar. Even though it was a cosmopolitan city where girls went to school, they did not play sports. Maria says she was seen as a bit of a freak of nature. Then one day her coach announced that they were sending her to a tournament to play girls from all over Pakistan! She joined the girls' national squash team and was soon traveling to tournaments throughout Pakistan and in other parts of Asia as well.

In 2006, as Peshawar and its surroundings were seething with terrorism and the Taliban were unleashing persistent, almost daily, bombings, Maria turned pro (huzzah!) and continued to play tournaments around the continent . . . training, traveling, winning medals, earning money for her family. Then she would come home to a place where everyone quite literally prayed to get through the day without carnage. Every time she left, she had to say goodbye knowing that it was entirely possible that she was saying goodbye for the last time.

In 2007, Toorpakai was excelling so much in squash that she was invited to receive an award of excellence from President Musharraf. She was the number one female squash player nationally. She was the first female to play in shorts and a T-shirt. She was an inspiration, but being an inspiration also meant you were dangerous. Not long after this monumental recognition, her father discovered a note affixed to his windshield: If Maria did not stop playing squash there would be dire consequences. Her picture with Musharraf in the newspapers had sealed her fate, and her name made her even more of a target. Her name provided evidence of her tribal roots, and the Taliban would not stand for a tribal girl being outside the four walls of her family home, much less becoming a national sports hero. She relates her experience in her memoir: "I come from the same bloodline and same tribe as the Taliban, and when they found out their own girl is playing in shorts and playing squash at that level, they just threatened us to death. They couldn't bear that."

Not wanting to put anyone at her training facility in danger but never even *considering* stopping, this incredible young woman decided to shut herself in her home, turn her mattress on its side, and continue to train there—against her bedroom wall. Aside from periodically sneaking out to travel to the occasional squash tournament—hiding under blankets in the back seat of their car, booking plane tickets only last minute or at the airport itself—she was confined for THREE YEARS. Oh, death threats, you say? Maria will just be in her bedroom NOT GIVING UP, THANK YOU.

Because of her severely compromised training, Maria the Great started to lose tournaments. She felt her bright future slipping away. Not only was her body suffering, but her mind and her mental state were crumbling as well. Watching his beloved daughter begin to lose her spark, Maria's father finally told her she could not continue to live in Pakistan and had to try to get to America. Even though she was a shell of her former self and was in no way the champion she had been, her father told her, "It's not about playing anymore, Maria. It's about staying alive."

With her sister's help, Maria began to email colleges, universities, academies, coaches, and squash camps all over the world. For more than two years Maria emailed people, informing them that she was the "sole and first ever Pakistani and tribal Pashtun girl to represent Pakistan in international squash tournaments, reaching the rank of #58 while securing the World Junior #3 title," and asking for their help . . . and nobody responded.

Then a beautiful, glorious, much-too-late-but-okay-maybe-right-on-time thing happened. A response to one of her hundreds of emails finally came! Jonathon Power, world champion squash player from Toronto (Canada represent!), had written her back. Power was the first North American to reach world number one ranking in the sport. He understood that a tribal Pashtun girl being a national champion was a miracle. He helped move Maria to Toronto, where he gave her a job at his academy and became her coach.

Ten months after arriving in Canada, in January 2012, after nearly a year of training, getting her body and mind back in shape, Power told her she was ready. He enrolled her in the Liberty Bell Open in Philadelphia. Maria was scared. What if she didn't have it anymore? What if she *wasn't* ready? Cut to: She won every one of her matches (Every. Match.) and snagged the title. She Skyped her family in Pakistan, showing off her trophy. Her dad, beaming, excitedly told her that the *Rocky* statue was only a twenty-minute walk from where she was staying in Philly.

I really, truly hope Maria jogged up those steps, just like Rocky, and raised her arms in triumph when she reached the top.

JOAN OF ARC

First, let's get the name thing out of the way. Joan's real name was Jehanne d'Arc. Or Jehanne Romée. Or possibly Jehanne de Vouthon. She didn't hail from a place called Arc, as the Anglicization of her father's surname, d'Arc, suggests. Joan grew up in Domrémy, a village in northeastern France. A devout Catholic peasant, Joan had no military training when she cut her hair off, donned men's clothing, and led French forces to defeat the English at the historic Battle of Orléans in 1429. She was eighteen years old and the name she gave to herself was simply Jehanne la Pucelle ("Joan the Maid").

The Battle of Orléans, also known as the Siege of Orléans, occurred during the Hundred Years' War (1337–1453)—a series of conflicts waged between the English House of Plantagenet and the French House of Valois over the right to rule the kingdom of France. Although primarily a dynastic conflict, the war

inevitably led to French and English nationalism. Fun tidbit: French, or rather, what is known as Anglo-Norman French, was the language of the kings and nobility of England for more than three hundred years. French was the native language of every English king from William the Conqueror (1066–1087) until Henry IV (1399–1413), whose mother tongue was English. His son, Henry V (1413–1422), was the first king of England since the Norman invasion who chose to speak English as his primary language. Before that, English was kind of thought of as a peasant language. Huh. So, even when we are looking back and saying these battles were between the English and the French, it is not the English and the French we know and love today. From what I can gather, the Hundred Years' War was two French dynasties battling it out for the kingdom of France, and one of those dynasties ruled England and was, therefore, considered "the English." Can you say confusing?

The Battle of Orléans (October 1428–May 1429) was the turning point in the war. France had been suffering some major defeats when a wunderkind from Domrémy showed up. For six months prior, the English and their French allies had appeared to be winning, but the siege collapsed nine days after Joan's arrival. Allow me to insert a little "BOOM" right here.

But I'm getting ahead of myself. In 1425, when Joan was about thirteen, she said that she began to hear voices she identified as Saint Michael, Saint Catherine, and Saint Margaret. Her angelic messengers were sent by God, relaying a mission of overwhelming importance: to save France by driving out its enemies and to install Charles the Dauphin as its rightful king. Can you imagine? The Hundred Years' War is going on, and here's our devout farm girl, barely a teenager, churning butter one day or whatever, and suddenly she's given a mission from God to SAVE FRANCE, and this powerhouse is like, YES, this makes sense to me, let's DO it. Joan of Arc is Beyoncé, that's all there is to it.

Modern scholars and physicians have suggested that Joan may have suffered from mental illness or epilepsy. Another theory is that she contracted bovine tuberculosis, which can lead to seizures and dementia, while working with cows on her family's farm. These scholars suggest that the voices she heard in her head, which told her to lead France to victory and guided her on every step of her incredible journey, were the result of illness. But that kind of makes me want to throw something across the room.

Here we have an inspired, fearless, pious young woman who hears voices—one might call that divine inspiration—telling her she's going to help win a war and get a king his crown. She seeks an audience with the dauphin, *which she achieves,* cuts off her hair, dresses in men's garb, and steers an army to quick victory. This girl was responsible for outlining military strategies, directing troops, and proposing diplomatic solutions to the English. So forgive me if I laugh in your face when you try to discount her with an epilepsy diagnosis.

Prophecies had been circulating for years about an armored maiden who was coming to save France, and that said maiden would come from the borders of Lorraine, where Domrémy, Joan's birthplace, is located. As a result, when word got out about Joan's attempts to see the dauphin, people were like, Holy crap, *she's here!* Joan did not disappoint. She so inspired the besieged citizens of Orléans that the people rose up alongside the army to help fight. This rock-star teen dispatched a famous missive to the English commanders ordering them, in the name of God, to "begone, or I will make you go." BUT OKAY, YEAH, I GUESS LET'S JUST WRITE HER OFF AS MENTALLY ILL.

Because of Beyoncé—I mean Joan—and her awesomeness, Charles was crowned at Notre-Dame de Reims in 1429, followed by a gradual reconquest of English-held French territories. In 1430, however, during the siege of Compiègne, Joan was captured by the Burgundians, French nobles allied

with the English, and accused of some seventy charges—the patriarchy was MAD—most of which related to her wearing men's clothing and claiming that God slid into her DMs. At her trial, she was accused of wearing her hair "cropped short and round like a young fop's" and, by wearing "the garments of a man, short, tight, dissolute," defying "Divine Law." She also carried and used weapons, which was unacceptable for women. In doing these things, according to the Church, Joan committed blasphemy. Charles, for whom Joan had fought so valiantly, made no attempt to save her.

Joan's trial began on January 13, 1431, in Rouen, Normandy, but she was not called to testify until February 21. Between February 21 and March 24, she was interrogated nearly a dozen times. According to the Historical Academy for Joan of Arc Studies, "In detailed testimony . . . witnesses related that Joan of Arc had told them that she had worn, and had resumed, this clothing and kept the hosen and doublet 'firmly fastened and tied together' because this provided her with the only means she had of protecting herself against the incidences of attempted rape which her English guards were inflicting on her." Joan protested during her trial that her wearing of men's clothes was in fact NOT in violation of the Church's laws, because when done for reasons of necessity—i.e., protecting oneself from sexual assault—it was considered sensible and allowable. She was like, *context*, guys, come on! Her judges did not agree.

Court transcripts translated from the French and Latin reveal that Joan was bold and strong in the face of her interrogators. Not only deeply religious and wholly committed to the path that God had laid out for her, she also seems to have had remarkable belief in *herself*. She could have saved herself. She could have said all the things those geezers wanted to hear, but she wouldn't. She didn't believe she had done anything wrong, and she held firm in her truth. She stood before these men, who held her life in their hands, and she dared to look straight in their faces and declare, "You say that you are my judge; I do not know if you are: but take good heed not to judge me ill, because you would put yourself in great peril. And I warn you so that if God punish you for it, I shall have done my duty in telling you." Mic. Drop.

She was initially sentenced not to death but to life imprisonment after signing a confession and agreeing to remove her men's clothing. But she rebelled, put the men's clothes back on, and told the court that her voices had returned. It was these two acts that earned Joan a conviction as a "relapsed heretic" and sent her to the stake. Incidentally, do you know what some other words for heretic are? Dissenter, nonconformist, freethinker, and iconoclast. Um, *yes, please.*

On the morning of May 30, 1431, at the age of nineteen, Joan was burned at the stake in a marketplace in Rouen. It is said that she had to be burned three times in order for her remains to be "fully burnt," that some of her organs, most notably her heart, resisted burning. While many believe this is the stuff of legend, the French scientist Philippe Charlier says it was common at the time. Organs hold a lot of water and cremating a body completely is no small task. Sure, facts are facts, but. . . her *heart* wouldn't burn. That is some poetry there.

About twenty years after Joan's execution, at the behest of her family, Charles VII ordered an inquiry into her trial. He may well have been motivated by a desire to clear her name so that his coronation and his reign were not forever linked to a condemned heretic. It took years for the retrial to commence, but finally, on the order of Pope Calixtus III, proceedings in 1455–56 led to Joan's sentence being revoked and annulled. While this was the moment when she was officially exonerated, it's important to note that the people of Orléans had held masses and processions in Joan's honor every year since her execution. They knew what was up. In 1909, Joan was beatified in Notre-Dame de Paris by Pope Pius X and canonized by Pope Benedict XV on May 16, 1920. She is the patron saint of France.

LOUISE AUGUSTINE GLEIZES

The word "hysteria" comes from the Greek word *hysterika*, meaning "uterus." That fact alone—I'm already mad. ARE YOU SERIOUS? The ancient Greeks thought hysteria was caused by a "wandering womb." If you're curious what that means, they literally thought a woman's uterus would become displaced and roam about the body, causing any number of unfortunate ailments. Sore throat? Uterus must be lodged in your throat. Constipated? Obviously, your uterus is stuck in your butt. You know . . . *science*. Because there was very little understanding of female biology, the term "hysteria" was used to describe a plethora of physical and emotional "female illnesses." The historian Mark Micale provides this shady spin:

"Hysteria has served as a dramatic medical metaphor for everything that men found mysterious or unmanageable in the opposite sex." By the way, you know what the Greeks advised as treatment for a wandering womb? Plentiful sex and constant pregnancy, of course! Keep that uterus (and lady) in its place by weighing it down with a baby.

Louise Augustine Gleizes was born in Paris on August 21, 1861. As was customary at the time, Louise was sent away to the country to live with a wet nurse (a woman who breastfed your baby for you) for the first nine months of her life. Using a wet nurse was common among the upper classes, who could hire someone to live with them, but by the nineteenth century in Paris, with more women entering the workforce, it became common among the working class as well. The un-rich were more likely to send an infant away to the countryside, where the conditions were not always great. One sister and two brothers of Louise died in their first fifteen months of life while living with a wet nurse. Oof. That is a horror film.

After a somewhat traumatic beginning, life continued to be hard for young Louise. She was once again sent away and spent time at a convent with some physically abusive nuns—more horror-movie shit. She was then raped by a family friend who was either her mother's lover or boss or both. All that happened before Louise had even reached her teen years.

As Gleizes got older, she began to suffer from convulsions. I mean, of course she did. When she was about thirteen, she was working full time because child labor laws were not a thing, and she began to act out sexually. No doubt this girl had been deeply affected by all the trauma she had suffered in her very young life. Her convulsions became more frequent, which led her mom to send her to L'Hôpital des Enfants Malades in Paris—the world's first-ever children's hospital—and after five months she was moved to La Salpêtrière Hospital's hysteric ward on October 21, 1875, at the age of fourteen.

The patriarch of the study of hysteria in the nineteenth century was the pioneering neurologist Jean-Martin Charcot. Even though Charcot didn't get everything correct, he is rightly respected and revered. What's known in America as Lou Gehrig's disease is known in France as Charcot's disease, as Charcot was the first to systematically describe it. He also transformed how the world looked at hysteria in general. Prior to Charcot's time, hysteria was seen as a wacky female affliction that did not warrant proper scientific investigation. In his eulogy of Charcot, Sigmund Freud stated, "The first thing that Charcot's work did was to restore its dignity to the topic." That all said, in addition to being revered, he also deserves a little side-eye.

Charcot initially surmised that hysteria was a neurological disorder for which patients were predisposed. Although he respected the ailment that his patients were suffering from, he had no interest in mental illness or anything in the psychological realm. His neurology blind spot meant that he observed his patients and their symptoms, but he did not actually *listen* to them. As described in Asti Hustvedt's *Medical Muses: Hysteria in Nineteenth-Century Paris*, if a woman was in the middle of a "hysterical attack" and began recounting details of a sexual assault or if she screamed for her mother, Charcot would make note of it as nonsense "noise." The scream was a symptom only. He never paid any mind to the *content* of the scream. Side note: That would come later with Freud, but don't get too excited.

Photography arrived at La Salpêtrière the same year Gleizes did. The hospital used photography, a relatively new technology, to document patients in various stages of a hysterical attack. Most likely due to her youth and her expressive face, Louise was the "hysteric" who was photographed the most in Charcot's ward. "The camera likes her," the hospital photographer, Paul Regnard, remarked.

Hysterical attacks, as observed by Charcot and his fellows, included expressions of uncontrolled emotions, auditory and visual hallucinations, sexual assertiveness, seizures, and eccentric physical contortions, which they called *attitudes passionelles*, or "passionate poses." Gleizes distinguished herself from other patients in the ward with her "execution" of the passionate poses. The photographs were supposed to display a series of these symptoms and provide evidence for Charcot's theories, but they did much more than that. Louise became a medical celebrity. The photographs of her became famous.

Stories of hysteria patients filled the newspapers in Paris. Crowds showed up weekly at the hospital for Charcot's demonstrations, in which he practiced hypnosis on the "hysterics"—he considered the ability to be hypnotized a clinical feature of hysteria. According to Judith Herman's *Trauma and Recovery*, "His Tuesday Lectures were theatrical events, attended by 'a multi-colored audience, drawn from all of Paris: authors, doctors, leading actors and actresses, fashionable demimondaines, all full of morbid curiosity.'" It was a hot ticket.

Soon these demonstrations became a full-on show, the patients became performers, and Charcot became the biggest celebrity of all, the ringmaster. Although Charcot attempted to stay objective, there's no question he loved the acclaim and was a bit of a showman. And while he was genuinely invested in making strides in the study of hysteria, it's clear he turned his patients into specimens to serve his own needs.

In light of what we know about the sexual and physical abuse Louise suffered as a child, having her "perform" her trauma and her supposed hysteria in front of an audience is already ethically problematic, but *hypnotizing* her, forcing her to do any number of things for the "audience," and then *using* it to say, "See, look how easily I hypnotized and controlled her . . . that proves she's a hysteric!" is all very what-the-fuck. Near the end of his life Charcot conceded that hysteria was actually a psychological affliction, not a neurological one. He also acknowledged that patients like Louise who had experienced trauma were simply more susceptible to the power of suggestion and hypnosis. His whole hysteria model was false.

One day in 1878, after three years in the hysteric ward, Gleizes recovered suddenly. "Sensibility completely restored," her file read. She was doing so well that she began working at the hospital as a *fille de service*, or a ward girl. What's shocking is that during the sixteen months that Louise worked and lived at the hospital, she continued to "perform" in Charcot's hysteric demonstrations. She was no longer symptomatic and no longer a patient, but it appears she allowed herself to be triggered through hypnosis so she could display hysteric symptoms, which is *really* odd because there was a ward full of patients with active symptoms, so what the hell was Charcot doing? I mean, we know what he was doing . . . he wanted his star. The photographs of Louise during this time show her not in her customary

hospital gown but in her hospital uniform. So, what, she'd clean up some bedpans and then be like, "Okay, Chloe, I'm just going to head down to the hysteric ward on my break for a quick hypnosis sesh!"

Sadly, after sixteen months, Louise relapsed. I can't help but think the hypnosis was like playing with fire for her, like poking the bear of her past traumas. Her medical records note that when she relapsed there was a change—she was angry and violent, she ripped apart a straitjacket, and for the first time ever, she was locked in a cell. Some say this behavior coincided with her desire to stop participating in Charcot's demonstrations. In her medical records, the translation from the French indicates that she no longer wished to be "a star." Perhaps the good doctor did not like that very much. I mean, it's entirely plausible that he did not want to lose his leading lady. I think she got fed up and wanted out and he did not want to let her go and then she relapsed. Badly. And that's when they locked her up. It's a mess. A low-down, dirty mess.

After two months in her cell, Louise had finally had enough and ripped the brackets from the windows and escaped. She was found outside and brought back, but they did not attempt to lock her up again. Soon after, she was truly ready to leave for good. The last dated entry in her file in 1880 reads, "On September 9, [Louise] escaped from La Salpêtrière, disguised as a man." When she was an infant, her family sent her away to a wet nurse, then they sent her away to a convent, then she was a child working full time at a place where she was sexually assaulted, AND THEN she was in a hospital at the mercy and in a sort of servitude to powerful men. Finally, having had enough, she disguised *herself* as a man—which was not only a transgressive act but an illegal one in Paris at the time—and nineteen-year-old Louise attained the one thing she had never had in her entire life: freedom.

Footnotes to Louise's medical records at La Salpêtrière indicate that after she left she was living with a lover—supposedly someone she met at the hospital—in a pied-à-terre near Notre-Dame. While we may not know exactly what happened to Louise, we do know what happened to her famous photographs. In 1928, the writers André Breton and Louis Aragon reprinted six photos of Louise in the publication *La Révolution surréaliste* to commemorate the fiftieth anniversary of hysteria. It seems the nineteenth-century hysterics were all the rage with the Surrealists: "We, Surrealists, who love nothing so much as those young hysterics, the perfect example of whom is supplied to us by the study concerning the delicious Augustine—admitted to the Salpêtrière in Dr. Charcot's care not yet 15." Really, dudes? Calling a troubled, "not yet 15"-year-old girl "delicious"?

It gets better: The invitation to the opening event of the 1938 Exposition Internationale du Surréalisme, overseen by Marcel Duchamp, promised attendees a night of *l'hysterie*. During the evening, visitors witnessed a performance by the actress Hélène Vanel, who was trained for the occasion by none other than Salvador Dalí. Vanel, in various states of undress, wildly splashed around in a man-made pond and eventually re-created a hysteria attack on a bed. A photo from the event makes clear their intention to link sex appeal with mental instability and female submission. Ugh.

It's hard to comprehend just how famous Louise was in late nineteenth-century Paris. The photographs of Louise went on to inspire books, plays, movies . . . and she unquestionably brought fame and acclaim to Charcot. She was his medical muse. Too often the woman who inspires and uplifts the man stays in the shadows, allowed only to exist in a little box labeled "muse." Louise literally ripped the brackets off the window of that box and said, "I'm done with this." Her escape says to me: I no longer consent to this. I DON'T CONSENT.

A WORD ABOUT FREUD

Of the five major case histories Freud published, his famous study of "Dora" was the only one of a female patient. "Dora" was Ida Bauer. Even though "hysteria" was a problematic and misogynistic diagnosis, one might imagine that Freud would be the guy to arrive on the scene and investigate the *psychological* aspect of the condition, moving beyond Jean-Martin Charcot's erroneous belief that it was a neurological disorder—pay attention to the content of the scream, as it were. What we find, however, when we look at this famous case is not an ally of women and their psychological traumas or ailments, but several dangerous precedents that still exist, more than 120 years later.

Dora's father brought her to Freud when she was a teenager after she had accused a family friend of sexual assault. According to Freud, Dora's father asked him to "please bring her to reason." Kate Novack, whose Oscar-shortlisted documentary *Hysterical Girl* examines Dora from a modern feminist perspective, points out, "So that, right off the bat, is the sort of trope of the young woman who comes forward and is told that she's being unreasonable. This [trope] is one that audiences today are unfortunately still very familiar with."

When Dora was thirteen years old, she was assaulted by a middle-aged friend of her father's who forced himself on her and kissed her. Freud's response was, "This was surely just the situation to call up a distinct feeling of sexual excitement in a girl." Instead, Dora had "a violent feeling of disgust, tore herself from the man," and left.

Freud goes on to surmise that this behavior from Dora was "already entirely and completely hysterical."

Filmmaker Novack continues, "What was actually more upsetting as I was doing the research was the degree to which the thought patterns behind his ideas in the case are still so present. When I went back and watched the Anita Hill testimony it's—they're talking about repression and fantasy and the idea of the woman who 'wanted it.' Some of those themes also came up in the [Christine] Blasey Ford testimony."

Instead of Freud investigating psychological responses to lived trauma, what we have is a physician concluding that a child of thirteen, after being sexually assaulted by her father's middle-aged friend, was *sexually excited* and that her VERY APPROPRIATE response of feeling disgusted and taking self-preserving action was evidence of hysteria. Freud may be the grandfather of psychotherapy, but he was also the person who popularized, or even invented, the idea that "women want it."

One of the important innovations that resulted from Freud's work in this area is the idea that psychological distress can lead to physical symptoms. The mind-body connection. But his theories also contributed to the persistent distrust of women's subjective reports of their own bodies. We see that play out again and again to this day. The all-too-common practice of ignoring women's symptoms, shrugging away their pain (even more prevalent with Black women), and even still labeling us as being "hysterical" (AND NOT IN THE FUNNY PHYLLIS DILLER WAY) is alive and well. Not only does a woman "want it," but her pain might also "all be in her head." So, while I am a HUGE fan of psychotherapy (shout out to my girl, Dr. Penelope!), Dr. Freud did not get everything right and we are still trying to dismantle some of the horseshit that sprang from his work.

ANNIE HINDLE AND
FLORENCE HINES

D rag kings. Where are they? Why do drag queens alone have their heels firmly planted at the center of pop culture while drag kings are almost nowhere to be found? I mean they exist . . . you just have to go looking for them. Drag kings certainly have grown in visibility, yet they remain on the margins of mainstream pop culture. Even though you probably don't know any drag kings by name and can't quote them to your friends at brunch, kings and those who were once called "male impersonators" have been around for more than a minute, pushing boundaries, entertaining enthralled fans, and making political statements. Please allow me to introduce you to two of the original originals.

ANNIE HINDLE

Annie Hindle was about twenty when she and her mother moved from their native England to the United States in 1868, putting down roots in Jersey City. Annie had already established herself as a performer in England, appearing mostly in provincial theaters where her act consisted of "serio-comic" songs performed as both female and male characters. When she arrived in America, she dropped the ho-hum female characters and doubled down on drag. Now "drag" wasn't a term that was in use back then, but she did describe herself as "the great seriocomic and impersonator of male characters." Don't you wish you could be a fly on the wall? A fly that is capable of time travel back to 1868? Why *exactly* did Annie drop the female characters from her act? Perhaps she discovered that no one else, not one other dame, was doing male impersonation in America and she knew she'd have a lock on the specialty? We may never know, but the reality is . . . Annie Hindle was the first male impersonator to appear on the American variety stage.

Before she left England, Hindle had the smarts and the where-withal to purchase promo ads for herself in the *New York Clipper*, a weekly entertainment newspaper, to promote her act in advance of her arrival. This self-promotion, coupled with the novelty of her act, was successful in creating buzz for herself: she had bookings within two weeks of landing in America. I love that she hyped herself before she and her mum had even stepped onto the steamer *City of Paris*, bound for New York, just *knowing* how fierce her act was. She was telling them: You don't even KNOW what's coming. And she was 100 percent correct. Here is an example of an ad she placed for her act in the *London Era* in 1864, as cited in Gillian Rodger's *Just One of the Boys*:

> *Look out, or, I'll warn you, Miss Annie Hindle, seriocomic and the greatest impersonator of male characters in the world, is creating the greatest sensation in Stockton ever known since the days of man. Hundreds crowd every evening to witness her wonderful change. Her wardrobe and make-up is certainly splendid and is much to her credit, as she is very young and striving to gain the good opinion of all, and no doubt in a little time she will have gained the top of her profession.*

Annie was the real deal. She specialized and excelled in portraying realistic male characters through song. Audiences were astonished by the authenticity of her performance and her low alto singing voice. According to Rodger, "She appeared to perform some kind of magic on the stage, transforming herself in ways that made her indistinguishable from male performers." At a time when women were seen as inherently different from men, Hindle blew people's minds nightly.

So, what was the act? Generally speaking, it consisted of three songs, performed as three different male characters. That meant three different outfits and looks—Hindle was known for how fast she could do her changes in the wings. In between each verse of each song, she would pause, interrupting herself to do little comic monologues, make puns, and, perhaps most exciting, do crowd work . . . all in character. I cannot stress enough how major this was for a woman of that era. I was struck by something Rodger wrote: "All male impersonators in American variety were exceptional women because they trespassed on the traditionally male ground of comedy." WOW. These are the great-grandmothers of female comedians—not only of drag kings but of Women in Comedy itself!

Her many talents made Hindle an instant hit among audiences, and for upward of a year on the American variety scene she was the only woman doing this kind of act. Several came after her, no doubt inspired by her and how full her booking calendar was, but Annie was the ORIGINAL. At the height of her popularity Hindle was highly paid and often outearned her male colleagues. We all know there aren't many professions where you can say that. Maybe porn and supermodels? And nineteenth-century cross-dressing variety performers, apparently.

Hindle was so beloved by audiences and such a reliable performer on any billing, that within a year of landing in America she was booking gigs more than a season in advance and her promo ads no longer needed those long descriptions of her talents. She began to be known simply as "The Great Hindle."

Okay. I've fallen and I can't get up. The Great Hindle? I mean . . . yes, please?

Being an itinerant performer must have been an incredibly lonely affair, especially for someone who had moved from one country to another and never really put down roots before hitting the road for work. Remarkably, Hindle married a LOT of people: two men and at least five women. Illegitimate though the same-sex marriages were, she married each of the women while dressed as one of her male characters and using the name Charles.

At first, I found these marriages funny, outrageous even. Was she collecting spouses? Was this a nineteenth-century thing? Was marriage more akin to "going steady" back then? But then I found it a bit sad. I pictured a lonely Hindle, a performer who was always on the road yet searching for a spouse to call "home." While her relationship choices do not define her, her queerness and her marriages are important. Here is another example of a woman doing what she wanted to do at a time when choices for women were limited, and using masculine garb as a way to gain access, to gain freedom. I want to marry these women, Hindle said to herself, so I'm going to throw on my show suspenders, call myself Charles, and, damn it, I'm going to marry these women.

As variety continued to flourish, enterprising male performers often took on the additional role of theatrical manager. It was generally not an option for female performers, but wouldn't you know it? In 1875, Annie Hindle defied the odds and took over as the manager of the Grand Central Varieties in Cincinnati, becoming the ONLY female variety performer-manager. I can imagine her dominating audiences night after night dressed as a man, soaking up the adulation, feeling that masc power, and coming to the realization that she could do anything the boys could do, including run a company. Unfortunately, Hindle chose to move into variety management at the absolute worst time, as the economy was plunging headfirst into what would become known as the Long Depression (1873–79). But like any woman in this book who tried and failed, for me the TRYING is the thing. Going forth where no woman had gone before to try? Hero status all day! The *New York Clipper* of course tried to blame poor management for Grand Central's demise, implying that a woman was unfit for the job. So, *not* a catastrophic economic depression that led to eighteen thousand American businesses going bankrupt. No, definitely her two X chromosomes though.

FLORENCE HINES

L egendary African American performer Florence Hines was known as "the queen of all male impersonators." In 1890, the *Indianapolis Freeman* called her "the greatest living female song and dance artist." Hines's star began to rise in the early 1890s, when she started to receive attention for her performances in Sam T. Jack's Creole Burlesque Company, also known as *The Creole Show*. The company was wildly popular and toured the United States and Canada, including a stint in Chicago during the 1893 World's Fair. Although it was produced by Jack, who was white, *The Creole Show* was a major milestone in Black performance in America because it turned the minstrel format on its head. The structure of the show may have been borrowed from the minstrel format, but the stage was no longer filled with white—and sometimes Black—performers in blackface, presenting what was

deemed as an authentic depiction of Black life. According to Black-theater historian Marvin McAllister, *The Creole Show* was "a major outlet for Black artists interested in cultivating nonminstrel material and developing a comedic tradition that was racially grounded but not riddled with stereotyping."

The Creole Show, which ran from 1890 to 1897, was innovative for many reasons. For one thing, the show was modern. It left the caricatures and the plantation settings behind and instead took place in an urban, sophisticated present. The cast was primarily women, which was spectacularly novel in and of itself, but even more revolutionary was that they were Black women. Black women whose talents as comedians, singers, and dancers were featured and celebrated. Another innovation lay in who portrayed the role of the "interlocutor," who was a sort of master of ceremonies. The interlocutor in *The Creole Show* was performed by a Black woman in male drag: Florence Hines.

As interlocutor, Hines performed a routine that was a send-up of the "dandy"—a stylish, modern young man who liked to imbibe and fraternize with women. The songs she sang played up the dandy's materialism and love of extravagance: "For I'm the Lad That's Made of Money," "Hi Waiter! A Dozen More Bottles," and "A Millionaire's Only Son."

When a white woman played a dandy, she got men in the audience to laugh at themselves or, if it was a working-class crowd, their betters. But when a Black woman played a dandy, it was a subversive act. Hines's witty and commanding interlocutor was a bold, statement-making departure from the derogatory portrayal of Black men in traditional minstrelsy, and an even further departure from the dim-witted "Mammies" or hypersexualized female characters that Black women were so often expected to play. Hines annihilated these stereotypes in her awe-inspiring performance.

Black burlesque and vaudevillian performances like Florence Hines's dandy hearken back to a tradition of transgressive Black pageantry first seen in the Pinkster and "Negro Election Day" festivals enslaved Black Americans celebrated earlier in the nineteenth century. According to the Africana professor and author Monica L. Miller, these festivals "featured parades and dances of slaves dressed to the nines in clothing normally reserved for their social and racial betters." These acts of playfulness and subtle mockery were encouraged by the enslavers, perhaps providing what Frederick Douglass described as "safety-valves, to carry off the rebellious spirit of enslaved humanity." More than fun and games, Miller explains, "for the participants, these events are a release from their . . . positions, at the same time they serve to increase the culture's awareness of the structural and social inequalities being mocked."

It's not a stretch to see a direct line between the pageantry and ribbing of these festivals and the captivating act that brought Hines so much acclaim, but the lineage would appear to continue all the way to the emergence of drag ball culture in 1920s Harlem, which inevitably led to the Black- and Latinx-dominated underground ballroom scene that flourished in the 1970s and '80s. In ball culture, performers routinely wore clothes associated with an alternate gender and with different social classes than their own, the goal being "realness" mixed with transgressive satire. One could posit that the performances and pageantry of those nineteenth-century festivals, *and* the dandy Hines portrayed, *and* the emergence of underground ball culture were all ways in which Black Americans could, as Miller puts it, "visualize dignity in the face of oppression."

But let's get back to Florence!

A review in the February 1892 Kansas City *American Citizen* proclaims that Hines "as a male impersonator is perfection itself. Improvement on Florence Hines' part is out of the question." The reviewer goes on to report that while Sam T. Jack may have had many imitators, his show and his company had no equals. In 1904, the *Indianapolis Freeman* reported that Hines "commanded the largest salary paid to a colored female performer." And in their book, *Out of Sight: The Rise of African American Popular Music, 1889–1895,* Lynn Abbott and Doug Seroff observe, "Hines's male impersonations provided the standard against which African American comediennes were compared for decades."

These few random—and thrilling—quotes are most of what we have to piece together a picture of Hines's life. Sadly, we don't know where or when she was born or how she got her start on the stage. Unlike her Caucasian counterparts, Hines likely was not profiled as frequently (if at all) in main-stream (white) publications, though she was successful with both Black and white audiences, making her a boundary-breaking trailblazer to be sure. According to queer historian Hugh Ryan, Florence, unlike her white peers, "seemed to have no personal publicity materials (or at least none that have been kept in archival collections)." The lack of information about Hines is disgraceful and really emphasizes the lack of care that has been given to Black stories, Black history, and Black people in America. I yearn to know everything there is to know about Hines, a grand dame of comedic and drag history, but the documentation simply is not there. It's a damn shame.

According to a letter to the editor that was published in the African American newspaper the *Chicago Defender* in 1920—the year Prohibition went into effect—Hines had become a preacher since her hometown of Salem, Oregon, had gone dry. If this letter is to be believed, it's worth considering that the talent to reach people and the desire to uplift them was really a central part of *both* paths Hines chose: the comedic stage performer and the preacher. I can see how Hines was preaching in her own way during her years in *The Creole Show*. Her performance provided its own kind of sermon for the audience, affirming that she was more than a stereotype, more than what society thought a Black woman should or could be. Florence Hines reportedly passed away in 1924. Like Annie Hindle, so many innovative and great artists stand on her shoulders. We are indebted to them.

OCTANDRIE; MONOGYNIE.

Bougainvillea.

2.

HISTOIRE NATURELLE, Botanique.

JEANNE BARET

Jeanne Baret was a skilled and ambitious young woman who moved beyond a life of rural poverty in the mid-eighteenth century and, disguised as a man, became the first woman to circumnavigate the globe. Jeanne was born in the Burgundy region of France in 1740 to father, Jean, a day laborer, and mother, Jeanne. I'm just gonna go out on a limb here and say the name Jean and all its variations was VERY popular at the time. For Jeanne and her people, illiteracy would have been the norm. Burgundy was one of the more backward provinces of France in terms of the condition of the peasant classes, and it is likely that Baret's family was quite impoverished. Those who traveled through the region during this period described the poverty with absolute incredulity.

Prior to the Industrial Revolution in the nineteenth century, the average European country dweller strayed no more than twenty miles from home. When you factor in her illiteracy and poverty, Jeanne Baret's story is all the more extraordinary, for Jeanne would go far beyond what her parents accepted as their lot in life and much farther than twenty miles from home—all the way around the world, in fact. Her life would lead her to cross gender *and* class barriers, something that was quite unheard of at the time.

At some point between 1760 and 1764, Baret met the recently widowed doctor and botanist Philibert Commerçon (also Commerson, because Anglos hate spelling things right) and became first his housekeeper, then his assistant, and eventually his lover. I mean . . . it happens.

Some say that Commerçon introduced Baret to botany, while others believe she was already a skilled herb woman by the time they met, taught by her family through largely oral rural traditions. You didn't need to be able to read or write to possess a gift in this area. They may have been poor, but her family lived on the land, and it's very likely that Jeanne Baret would have developed an intimate relationship with it.

With stories like Jeanne's, where there are a LOT of missing pieces, it can be a bit dangerous when historians and authors fill in the blanks, sometimes wanting a historical figure to fit neatly into the story *they* wish to tell. With Jeanne, some writers desire to tell the story of an impoverished illiterate girl whom Commerçon saved, showing her the ways of botany, teaching her to read and write, and then bringing her on the adventure of a lifetime. Others push the narrative of an illiterate farm girl who was preternaturally gifted as an herb woman, and that it was *she* who taught the good doctor a thing or two. I think it's rarely black and white, and more than likely it's a mix of all the stories rolled up into one.

In 1766, after a series of defeats in the Seven Years' War, France was yearning to regain some prestige, to metaphorically reinflate its enfeebled penis. King Louis XV agreed to a costly round-the-world expedition—the first of its kind for France and only the fourteenth ever at that point—headed by Louis Antoine de Bougainville. That surely would be the dose of Viagra France needed to pump up the jams. The expedition was to be as much a display of power and leadership as a practical undertaking of discovery. It was the first voyage to circumnavigate the globe with professional naturalists and geographers aboard. The king awarded Commerçon the role of expedition botanist and he was directed to "make all the observations and relative discoveries on the coasts and even in the interior of the various countries."

Often in poor health and never having traveled on a ship, let alone lived at sea for two years, Commerçon would need an assistant and decided to take Jeanne. Since women were strictly forbidden aboard French naval ships, Jeanne disguised herself as a man and became "Jean." There are many theories about why Commerçon took Jeanne. It seems likely that he saw a skill in her and, I'm guessing, a passion for botany and discovery. He was also unwell and could trust her to care for him without making him feel like shit about it. They were also lovers, so there's that. Honestly, I picture them as a couple of horny science nerds wigging out over plants and shit.

Setting sail for two years with a bunch of dudes wouldn't have been a proposition to take lightly. Not to mention that the workload Jeanne was taking on was MASSIVE. You would have to have a passion for the work you were doing—there's no way it was just about following a man. Jeanne clearly possessed not only a thirst for adventure but also bravery and chutzpah. And, yes, she might also have been a bit horny for Philibert, too, even with that ridiculous name. It seems like a crazy idea, and I love that she was like: YES.

The ships assigned for the voyage were the frigate *La Boudeuse*, which carried about two hundred crew members, and the slower supply ship *Étoile*, with just over one hundred on board. For two years Jeanne's floating home was the *Étoile*, which one historian noted would have been the size of a townhouse. A townhouse? With a hundred other people? I'm sorry, *what?* I don't really fancy sharing a bed with someone I *like* . . . one hundred people in a townhouse sounds like a nightmare. One ray of light was that, because of all the equipment they had brought, the *Étoile*'s captain, François de la Giraudais, offered up his quarters to Commerçon and "Jean." That would have meant THEIR OWN BATHROOM, and that information just makes my sphincter unclench. A place where she could release her boobs each day from their wrappings? A private spot to poop? A sanctuary where one could retire for one's semi-regular cry? Perfect.

The *Étoile* departed from Rochefort, France, in December 1766, and met up with *La Boudeuse*, on which Bougainville was sailing, in Rio de Janeiro in 1767. Commerçon was not doing great, suffering from recurrent seasickness and a nasty leg ulcer. Baret would have spent most of her time attending to him. When they reached Rio, Commerçon was confined to the ship because of his leg. According to his memoirs, it appears that Baret did much of the specimen collecting (i.e., the *discovering*), hauling everything back to him on the ship. Some believe it was Jeanne and not Commerçon who first discovered what came to be known as the bougainvillea, a beautiful fuchsia vine— the likes of which I walk under every morning on my dog walk here in Los Angeles—that was named after the captain of their voyage and was surely their greatest discovery. Although Commerçon described the bougainvillea in his writings and gave it its name, he never published the plant. Bougainvillea was not officially documented until 1789, by Antoine Laurent de Jussieu, a French botanist, who used Commerçon's specimens and notes, but nowhere was there any mention of Jeanne Baret, making her contribution in this

discovery completely lost to history. Even though we may not be privy to all the details, to erase her entirely, giving her no credit when she was the one out there doing the legwork and schlepping specimens back to an ailing Commerçon . . . well, it's depressing yet all too common when it comes to the contributions of women being overlooked, ignored, or erased. After all, she was not *officially* there on that voyage, was she?

It seems there were some on the ship who suspected Jeanne was a woman. Maybe some of them knew her secret but didn't care. Or maybe they were too busy not dying of scurvy or trying to find the best (only?) bathroom where people couldn't hear them shitting. Yes, I am consumed with private spaces in which to poop, welcome to me. According to Bougainville's journals, it was when they got to Tahiti that Jeanne's true identity became known. She and Commerçon remained on the ship for a time afterward, but when they got back to French territory, Mauritius, they disembarked. Maybe

Bougainville did not want to face punishment for having a woman on board, and Commerçon's health may have been an issue, too. Perhaps it was best for all involved for the weird nerd plant couple to depart the expedition.

Baret spent seven years in Mauritius, and check this out: While Commerçon's financial resources on the island dwindled, Baret seems to have established herself independently, because records show her being granted property in Port Louis in 1770. Commerçon died in Mauritius in 1773 at the age of forty-five, and after his death Baret ran a tavern in Port Louis. On May 17, 1774, she wed Jean Dubernat, an officer in a French colonial regiment (ANOTHER JEAN—WHAT THE HELL). By the time she married, Jeanne was wealthy enough that SHE required a prenuptial contract. WHOA! She and hubs arrived back in France likely in 1775, thus completing her round-the-world trip and making her the first woman known to circumnavigate the globe. Huzzah! They settled in Dubernat's native village and bought property with Jeanne's fortunes.

Once Baret was back in France, Commerçon's family honored her contract and paid her for her services, and in 1785 Baret was granted a pension of two hundred livres a year by the Ministry of the Navy. The document granting her this pension makes clear the high regard with which she was held:

Jeanne Barré, by means of a disguise, circumnavigated the globe on one of the vessels commanded by Mr de Bougainville. She devoted herself in particular to assisting Mr de Commerçon, doctor and botanist, and shared with great courage the labours and dangers of this savant. Her behaviour was exemplary and Mr de Bougainville refers to it with all due credit. . . . His Lordship has been gracious enough to grant to this extraordinary woman a pension of two hundred livres a year to be drawn from the fund for invalid servicemen and this pension shall be payable from 1 January 1785.

Clearly, Bougainville did not prosecute or punish Baret for posing as a man and recommended she receive a pension! Her skill and her contributions were obviously highly valued, though, again, she never got official credit for any of the work she did with Commerçon, who has more than seventy species of plants named in his honor, carrying the epithet *commerçonii*. In spite of her astounding bravery, pioneer spirit, and lasting contributions to botany, there are no species named for Baret. She was involved with collecting more than six thousand plant specimens on the voyage, many of which are now housed in herbariums at the Muséum National d'Histoire Naturelle in Paris, and she is not credited for a single one. When I searched the museum's website for Commerçon's name, there he was, listed alongside many a plant, but nowhere is there mention of Jeanne Baret or any variation on her name. "Your search yielded no results!" Yeah, no kidding.

If it wasn't for Bougainville's brief mention of her in his memoir, Jeanne may have been entirely forgotten. She pops up in a few other places, but it's always as a footnote in the biographies of "great men." The Prince of Nassau-Siegen, who was a paying passenger on the expedition, wrote about Jeanne in his journals: "I want to give her all the credit for her bravery, a far cry from the gentle pastimes afforded her sex. She dared confront the stress, the dangers, and everything that happened that one could realistically expect on such a voyage. Her adventure should, I think, be included in a history of famous women." I like this guy.

Trying to fit Baret into a comfy, tidy box will not do. She was an entirely unique, independent, and surprising woman. She started as an illiterate peasant girl. She became literate, learned botany, and made sizable discoveries. She circumnavigated the globe and became financially independent. She owned property. She made her own way. Talk about going beyond twenty miles from home.

Jeanne Baret: a footnote no more.

ANONYMOUS WAS
A WOMAN

When we look at the women who dressed as men throughout history to gain access and opportunity or, hell, to be left alone, a different sort of disguise must also be considered: female writers who chose to write anonymously or pseudonymously. All told, "disguise" isn't quite the right word, since what we come to see is that it isn't a one-size-fits-all situation. There are various contexts and reasons why a woman writer might choose a different moniker or none at all. But hold up—let's ease into this one because it's a biggie.

In Virginia Woolf's *A Room of One's Own* (1929), the striking mantra that Woolf repeats is that a woman must have money and a room of her own if she is to write. The anger and the sharp subtle humor of this brilliant woman speak to us through the ages and pages of *Room*. The book is based on two lectures

Woolf delivered at Newnham and Girton, women's constituent colleges at Cambridge University, in 1928.

The constituent part is important here. In the 1870s, women were permitted to attend lectures at Cambridge, but they had to apply for special permission from each individual lecturer. Women won the right to sit for exams in 1881, but it wasn't until 1948 that they were awarded actual degrees, and that was hard won. They tried and tried over the years, but honestly, the men freaked the fuck out. A photo from 1897 featured in a BBC.com story about the history of women at Cambridge shows a massive protest by male undergraduates, all dressed in formal attire, wearing hats like fine gentlemen. In the photo these chaps are mutilating a female effigy in a courtyard at Cambridge, protesting women's rights to attend Cambridge as their equals. So that's fun. As Woolf says in *Room*, "The history of men's opposition to women's emancipation is more interesting perhaps than the story of that emancipation itself."

One of the most noteworthy moments in *Room* is the now-iconic introduction Woolf makes to Shakespeare's fictitious sister, Judith, who never stood a chance to exist in the first place. Even if she was witty, a keen observer, passionate about life, art, and humanity, even if she had all the gifts Shakespeare himself had, none of it would have mattered because Judith would not have been sent to get an education or tended to by tutors. She would have been tending to mutton stew or learning how to cross her ankles under her skirt so as to not create an unbecoming divot. And that was on a busy day. While Judith's passion tries to win out, with her limited (nonexistent) support system, she inevitably succumbs to the depths of unrealized genius, unwanted brilliance, and—super dark here—she would kill herself. As Woolf paints it, "She lies buried at some crossroads where the omnibuses now stop outside the Elephant and Castle." Oof.

The other iconic moment in *Room* is when Woolf proposes that Anonymous was a woman. Like poor Judith, Woolf refers to the "suppressed poet," the woman who didn't dare write all that was inside her, and she ventured "that Anon, who wrote so many poems without signing them, was often a woman."

It's a compelling idea, but of course it's not true. Not every writer who ever signed their work "Anon" was female, and it would be impossible to know what percentage of them were. In the eighteenth century, it was considered in bad taste for anyone, even a man, to publish what they had written, but it seems it was doubly unacceptable for a woman. It was considered immodest and embarrassing. The "doubly unacceptable" part is key here because the horror of a woman being immodest continued well after the eighteenth century. There were simply too many ramifications for a woman who had opinions, not to mention one who dared to write them down or advertise them in some way. Woolf elucidates sarcastically, "Publicity in women is detestable. Anonymity runs in their blood. The desire to be veiled still possesses them. They are not even now as concerned about the health of their fame as men are, and, speaking generally, will pass a tombstone or a signpost without feeling an irresistible desire to cut their names on it." Ha! One can't help but think of a place in the twenty-first century called the internet where a woman who has an opinion, and has the gall to state it, is often met with harassment and even death threats. How little has changed when we have simply moved from unsigned pages to locked Twitter accounts where the wolves are blocked from coming to eat us. Some days "Anonymous" looks very attractive.

According to the British historian James Raven, 80 percent of novels published between 1750 and 1790 were published anonymously. It was the default. I was shocked to discover that most English novels in the eighteenth century were written by women, many of whom published using their real names. These were not "fringe" writers; rather, they were *central* to the rise of the novel. Nonetheless, the authors who are most talked about from that time, the ones we remember and deem canon worthy, are almost all men.

Despite the contributions of women, no novel from that time period that was written by a woman has the canonical stamp on it. It seems that certain Very Important Scholarly Types had opinions and made decisions that led to textbooks being written and curriculums made . . . and suddenly an entire generation of writers was dismissed and largely forgotten. For example, Ian Watt famously declares in *The Rise of the Novel* (1957) that even though the majority of eighteenth-century novels were written by women, it was "a purely quantitative assertion of dominance," and, he seems to say, it was only Jane Austen's arrival on the scene in the nineteenth century that showed us that women could be great writers, too. Ugh. Watt's study, considered the seminal work on the origins of the novel, influenced a generation of scholars and untold curriculums. In response, we can hear the great seventeenth-century writer Aphra Behn, of whom Woolf said, "All women together ought to let flowers fall upon the tomb of Aphra

Behn . . . for it was she who earned them the right to speak their minds," rolling in her grave and muttering, "Well, fuck my drag."

Now, allow me to host you at my salon, a meeting of the minds where you will get to meet a handful of brilliant women writers who wrote anonymously or using a pseudonym or sometimes both.

———————

It's not breaking news that people the world over are obsessed with Jane Austen. There are countless biographies, museums, websites, and film adaptations of her work. The world has a wide-on for Jane, and you can count me in with that lot. Jane is the shit. The irony of Austen's superstar status, however, is that all her works were published anonymously during her lifetime. Her first novel, *Sense and Sensibility*, which was published (at her own expense, by the way) in 1811, was simply "By a Lady." Her next novel, *Pride and Prejudice*, was "By the Author of *Sense and Sensibility*." I love that Jane rejected both "Anonymous," which was still commonplace, *and* the use of a pseudonym. She wished to write, she wished to publish her work, she wished to be read. But she did not wish to be known, or at least it was not yet customary to be known, especially for a woman. But she also had no interest in hiding the fact that she was a woman. "By a Lady" is impressive.

Austen, in her anonymity, released book after book, each one going into multiple printings. *Sense and Sensibility, Pride and Prejudice, Mansfield Park, Emma* . . . what a run! Following Austen's death in July 1817, at the age of forty-one, the novels *Persuasion* and *Northanger Abbey* were published posthumously as a set, again without an author's name. Jane's brother Henry,

JANE AUSTEN

however, contributed a "Biographical Notice" to the set that, for the first time ever, identified Jane as the author of the novels.

Though Austen's work went out of print for a time after she died, her six finished novels were revived in 1832 and have never been out of print since. Some feel Henry unfairly "outed" Jane, while others believe what he did was a loving eulogy, a tribute to his gifted sister. The thing that stands out for me is that the only time a woman in the nineteenth century was entirely safe to be known as an author—a *great* author—was when she was in fact dead and in the ground and could no longer be accused of boasting.

Mary Shelley's *Frankenstein* was published anonymously on January 1, 1818, with a preface by Mary's poet husband, Percy Bysshe Shelley. To this day there are those who argue that PBS, not Mary, penned the classic, one of the arguments being that a nineteen-year-old *girl* could not have written such a work. *Frankenstein*, whose monster has no name, making him also anonymous, was both panned and celebrated in its day. Reviews aside, it is one of the most influential novels of our time.

MARY SHELLEY

Mary's mother was the great feminist philosopher and pioneer Mary Wollstonecraft, author of *A Vindication of the Rights of Woman* (1792) and someone we already know very well from the chapter on Margaret King! One wonders what Wollstonecraft, who was a spirited advocate for the education and advancement of women—and who boldly stamped her name on everything she ever wrote—would have thought of her daughter publishing a sensational book and not attaching her name to its cover and pages. Alas, Mary Wollstonecraft could respond with neither disappointment nor understanding because she died from complications following childbirth ten days after Mary junior was born.

After *Frankenstein*'s first printing, Mary Shelley agreed to put her name on subsequent editions and, one hopes, bask a little in its success. Mary Shelley was far more prolific than she is given credit for. She is so much more than *Frankenstein*, having written five other novels, a novella, and a great many poems, plays, and short stories. It's also important to note that despite the success of *Frankenstein*, Mary was not rich. After her husband's death, she worked tirelessly to support herself and her only surviving child with writing and editing jobs. Fiona Sampson observes in *The Guardian*, "The archives are full of her unsuccessful attempts to pitch to publishers. It's hard to imagine a male author who had experienced similar popular and critical success being so consistently knocked back."

By the time I first became aware of *Frankenstein*—I can't recall how old I was—it was never called simply *Frankenstein*. As far as I can remember, it has always been referred to as *Mary Shelley's Frankenstein*, which has got to be some beautiful just-deserts recompense for the novel first being published with no name at all. Even though you would think that the name "Mary" couldn't possibly be mistaken for a man's name, I distinctly remember questioning as a young person whether Mary Shelley was a boy or a girl. Why? Probably because the book so prominently touted HER NAME in the title: *Mary Shelley's Frankenstein*. Even young Tracy in modern times, all loud-mouthed and feminist, was marred by internalized misogyny and the ever-present patriarchy. I couldn't believe "they" would let a woman's name so boldly, so triumphantly be in the title of a legendary book from "the olden days." Listen, I'll be the first to admit I was brainwashed back then. The patriarchy is a powerful drug!

As we move from the eighteenth century to the nineteenth and twentieth, we see more and more female writers, poets, and playwrights begin to crop up, but a new kind of anonymity emerges: the pseudonym, or nom de plume. And lest we think such a thing occurred only in days gone by, we need only remember that it wasn't that long ago that Joanne Rowling was told by her publishers that her female-sounding name would simply not do for a book hoping to find a young male audience. Of course, it wasn't a choice made out of safety concerns for the author—no one in 1997 was going to accuse a woman of being an immodest trollop because she wrote a book. No, it was about *sales*. But that doesn't change the fact that the decision was steeped in misogyny! If you say you don't want to scare off little boy wizard readers with a female name . . . that's a *problem*, and boy oh boy does it send an ugly message to your little *girl* readers.

———

GEORGE SAND

*A*mantine Lucile Aurore Dupin was born in Paris in 1804 and was one of the most popular writers in Europe during her lifetime. Published in 1832, *Indiana* was the first novel she wrote on her own—she had previously collaborated with French author Jules Sandeau—and it was released under her pseudonym, George Sand. *Indiana*'s story critiques the laws surrounding women's equality in France. The titular character cannot leave her husband because she lacks the protection of the law: Under the Napoleonic Code, women could not claim ownership of their children or file for divorce. By February

1833, Sand began to be mentioned in the English press and referred to as "she," but it's unclear when and how it became known that she was a woman. As her literary star began to rise, critics often joked about her being female while also admitting that she was a literary phenomenon. I guess they couldn't get past a woman calling herself "George." Or was it because she was a phenom who was also a woman that they felt the need to mock, to puff themselves back up again?

Sand was known for her many love affairs and for scandalously smoking tobacco in public. She was also one of many notable nineteenth-century women who chose to wear male attire in public. Check this out: In 1800, the Parisian authorities issued an order requiring women to apply for a permit to wear "male" clothing—basically, trousers. The order declared that "any woman who wishes to dress as a man" (*toute femme désirant s'habiller en homme*) must present herself to the governing body for authorization. To do so, she needed the notarized signature of a health official declaring that the clothing was medically necessary. *Really.*

You'd be correct if you guessed that Sand did *not* comply. Wearing trousers was not only comfortable, but think of the basic benefit it provided, so deeply and simply feminist in nature: It allowed someone to move about more easily and freely. It's so simple. Freedom to *move*. This law remained in effect for 213 years. That's right: it was not officially repealed until 2013.

In Chicago in 1964, code 192-8 was passed, stating, "Any person who shall appear in a public place in a dress not belonging to his or her sex, with intent to conceal his or her sex, shall be fined." Oh, excuse me, is that a typo? You must mean 1864, yes? No, madam, I do not. You see, if you were a woman wearing "fly front pants," you were impersonating a man and could be fined and more than likely taken away in a police cruiser. The law was used to justify raids on lesbian and gay bars. To be clear, a woman *could* wear pants, but the zipper had to be in the back, because those were *women's* pants. Older lesbians recount tales of patrol wagons being lined up outside the bars and rushing to the back to turn their pants around before an officer shined his flashlight on their crotches to protect the good people of Chicago. Although gay bars were not illegal, zipper placement became an obsessive way to police women's bodies, their sexuality, and their lives.

Sand was highly respected by the literary and cultural elite in France, where her sex was known. Victor Hugo, Eugene Delacroix, Gustave Flaubert, and Honore Balzac sang her praises, but rest assured, not all her contemporaries admired her or her writing. The poet Charles Baudelaire wrote, "She is stupid, she is heavy, she talks too much; her ideas on morals have the same depth of judgment and the same delicacy of feeling as a janitor or a kept woman. . . . The fact that there are men who could become enamored of this latrine is indeed proof of the degradation of the men of this century." Wow, what crawled up his butt? George Sand was not hiding behind a pseudonym; hers was a deliberate choice, a rebranding, if you will. Of course, we can't escape the ever-present patriarchy and the gender discrimination that may have contributed to her choices, but it was obviously more nuanced than that.

CHARLOTTE, EMILY, AND ANNE BRONTË

Just as the vast majority of people are not aware that Austen published strictly anonymously in her lifetime, most people don't know that the Brontë sisters published exclusively under male pen names while they were living. The sisters were intellectually curious and demonstrated a gift for writing at a young age. Along with their brother, Branwell, they created entire worlds and printed tiny books for themselves. The family was not wealthy, and prospects for women at that time were essentially governess, schoolteacher, wife, lonely spinster, or some combination thereof. All three girls pursued teaching and governess work. Charlotte even considered opening a school for girls, though it never came to pass. Never one to hide her ambitions, Charlotte was not interested in playing the game of female humility and self-deprecation. In one of her letters, she wrote that she wished to be "forever known" as a writer, which makes it all the more curious that she never published under her real name.

In 1837, when Charlotte was twenty, she wrote to the poet laureate Robert Southey asking him to mentor her and sent him several poems she had written in his style. Southey wrote back after several months that "literature cannot be the business of a woman's life, and it ought not to be. The more she is engaged in her proper duties, the less leisure will she have for it even as an accomplishment and a recreation." Charlotte is most famous for writing *Jane Eyre*, but I will go on record that her response to Southey may be my favorite thing she ever wrote! Word on the street is that he didn't even pick up on her sarcasm. "In the evenings, I confess, I do think, but I never trouble anyone else with my thoughts. I carefully avoid any appearance of preoccupation and eccentricity, which might lead those I live amongst to suspect the nature of my pursuits."

She reassured Southey, "I have endeavoured not only attentively to observe all the duties a woman ought to fulfil, but to feel deeply interested in them. I don't always succeed, for sometimes when I'm teaching or sewing I would rather be reading or writing; but I try to deny myself." She wrapped up her devilishly delicious missive with a bang. "Once more allow me to thank you with sincere gratitude. I trust I shall nevermore feel ambitious to see my name in print; if the wish should rise, I'll look at Southey's letter, and suppress it." HAHAHAHAHA I LOVE HER.

The Brontë sisters' first book was a joint publication: *Poems by Currer, Ellis, and Acton Bell* (1846)—C for Charlotte, E for Emily, and A for Anne (way to spoil yourselves . . . take that first initial, gals!). The following year each sister produced a book: Charlotte's *Jane Eyre* (published under the name Currer Bell), Emily's *Wuthering Heights* (her only finished novel, published under the name Ellis Bell), and Anne's *Agnes Grey* (published under the name Acton Bell). *Jane Eyre* exploded onto the scene and became immensely popular; her publisher sent stacks of notices and messages for "Mr. Bell" to their family home. Charlotte finally had to come clean to her oblivious father, but she kept up all correspondence with her publishers as "Currer." When rumors began circulating that ALL the works by the Brontës came from a single pen, Charlotte and Anne traveled to London to stand before Charlotte's publisher, George Smith, and let him know that his bestselling author Currer Bell was, in fact, one woman: Charlotte. Although shocked, Smith was eager to fête Charlotte and Anne—to host them, take them to the opera, invite other authors who were fans of *Jane Eyre* to sup with them. Charlotte refused, insisting that they revealed themselves only to prove the rumors wrong. In a letter to her friend Mary Taylor, she wrote, "To all the rest of the world we must be 'gentlemen' as heretofore." What a kick in the arse and a tragedy, to refuse being fêted and lauded in the flesh. She wouldn't have had to pay for a single dinner! It's a bit depressing, especially given everything that's documented about Charlotte's wonderful ambitions.

Emily died one year after the publication of *Wuthering Heights* and Anne died two years after the publication of *Agnes Grey*. Charlotte was the last of her siblings to die, yet she made it only to thirty-eight. Brilliant Charlotte made uncommon choices for a woman of her time, most notably that she did not marry until she was thirty-seven. She soon became pregnant, finally embracing this long-put-off traditional role for women. And, wouldn't you know it, her health rapidly declined, and experts believe she died from dehydration and malnourishment caused by a complication of pregnancy called "hyperemesis gravidarum." Ambition, writing, and creating, all thought to be "men's work," allowed Charlotte to live. When she at last embraced what so many deemed "women's work," it inevitably killed her.

———————

The year 1819 saw the birth of two female babies who would go on to become two of the most iconic women of the nineteenth century. Even though one was born in a palace and one on a farmstead, like every other female baby born at that time, their lives would be pretty much laid out for them and only the most limited ambitions were possible. Girls were expected to be wives and mothers and not much else. Well, that is not what happened to either of these two babies! Alexandrina Victoria would become Queen Victoria and literally go on to define an era. Mary Anne Evans would go on to become George Eliot, one of the most celebrated writers in the world and the author of *Middlemarch*, which many believe is the greatest British novel of all time.

In addition to their birth year and their truly unexpected elevation to fame, Victoria and Eliot were both born to older fathers who were really counting on these late-in-life babies being boys . . . you know, because of all the ways a boy could *pay off* by being a person who *accomplishes* things and stuff like that. Aw, hell, too bad these two old dads only got a QUEEN and a GENIUS.

Queen Victoria became a fan of her birth twin, favoring the "healthy" moral tone that pervaded Eliot's work. Her Majesty even commissioned paintings of scenes from Eliot's books to be hung in Buckingham Palace. Because of the scandals that would beset Eliot—most notably, that she chose to live with a married man—the two were never able to meet in the flesh. But how spectacular would a fantasy stage play be about a secret meeting between them in, say, 1859, the year they both turned forty and Eliot published her first novel, *Adam Bede*? Fetch me a pen!

Arguably, Eliot's entire life was a bit of a scandal, starting with having a father who believed in educating his daughters. The story goes, and I don't know if I fully buy it but . . . because she was not considered attractive, Eliot's father thought her marriage prospects slim, so he decided to invest in an education not afforded many girls at that time. Again, not sure how I feel about the "you're ugly so you can be smart" take, but maybe it's because I see myself? Like, did my sense of humor develop because I wasn't considered "pretty"? I used to kid that God gave me jokes, not boobs. If I'd had both I would have been intolerable.

After establishing herself as an editor and a critic at the *Westminster Review* in London—where everything she wrote was published anonymously—Eliot desired to write fiction. While there were women writing under their own names in the mid-1850s, she was comfortable with anonymity and, at the same time, yearned to distance herself from "women's writing." She decided to use a pseudonym. It also helps to have a pen name when you want to shield your private life from public scrutiny because you're openly living with someone else's husband. Since she could not take her married lover's surname legally, she opted to take his given name, George, instead. And so, the pseudonym George Eliot was born.

Knowing that she shared her life with a married man, it's intriguing that Eliot was known for moralism in her work. Her novels often present a moral dilemma for her characters, which was very much in keeping with the Victorian novel. The choice that needs to be made is never easy or clear cut, but her narratives always seem to arrive at a similar conclusion: Acting in self-interest is . . . bad. Yet didn't she act in self-interest? Equally as pervasive in her writing are the themes of sympathy and compassion. According to Eliot, "The greatest benefit we owe to the artist, whether painter, poet, or novelist, is the extension of our

GEORGE ELIOT

sympathies." The artist, she insists, helps us see things from a different perspective, helps us develop compassion.

In 1857 and again in 1859, rumors began to circulate that George Eliot was in fact some guy from Warwickshire named Joseph Henry Liggins. The rumors were circulating because that's what Liggins was telling everyone. If Eliot wanted to stay hidden, Liggins would be happy to accept dinner invitations, and even donations from wealthy patrons, in the name of George Eliot. As described by biographer Kathryn Hughes, the Liggins uproar "had turned from a bit of unpleasant gossip into a concerted effort by enemies to strip her of every happiness." Eventually, Eliot had no choice but to reveal herself. Suddenly, everyone knew who she was, after years of being published anonymously and accepting her praise in parcels from the little pockets of people who discovered the truth along the way. She was now center stage, for better or worse. And it really wasn't worse. Book sales did not diminish, they soared! Eventually, Liggins faded into obscurity, but it was a good couple of years of turmoil and confusion. An angry editorial in the *Athenaeum* in 1859 claimed the whole imbroglio with Liggins "was a mystification, got up by George Eliot" to boost book sales, essentially accusing George Eliot of pretending to be Joseph Liggins!

When I think of Louisa May Alcott, who published *Little Women* in 1868 under her real name, I think of the opening scene in Greta Gerwig's 2019 film adaptation. The character of Jo, with ink-stained hands, sits in front of a publisher who agrees to print the short story she's just presented him on behalf of her "friend."

LOUISA MAY ALCOTT

After haggling about the price, the publisher asks Jo whose name he should attach as the author. Jo replies, "Oh, yes—none at all if you please." The movie plays with timelines, but the scene is taken from the original book and likely straight from Alcott's life. Just like Jo, young Alcott in her early salad days as a writer made money to send to her family by selling racy, pulpy stories such as "Pauline's Passion and Punishment." And like Jo, she sold such stories anonymously. According to the scholar and rare-book dealer Leona Rostenberg, "By her own admission, Louisa Alcott enjoyed writing tales injected with the 'lurid' not only because of the lucrative rewards, which she sorely needed, but because of her passion for wild adventurous life and even melodramatic action." She also realized that publishing such tales "would not enhance her reputation," so hiding her identity was necessary.

Alcott published her work anonymously, under a pseudonym, and using her real name. To protect her identity while selling these titillating and good-for-the-pocketbook tales, Alcott eventually graduated from being anonymous to using the gender-neutral pen name A. M. Bernard. Some may insist that Alcott had choices, she wrote under her real name: progress! True, but what she published under her own name was the pretty, palatable stuff. Alcott enjoyed the racy, bloody tales she was crafting, but she couldn't imagine a world where she could have her real name attached to both the lovely, soft stories as well as the lurid, fun stuff. As Rostenberg tells it, her pulpy publishers *wanted* her to use her real name, but she refused. While it was probably a *writer* thing rather than a *woman* thing, one can't escape the modesty aspect, for it was indelibly sewn into the fabric of being a woman. The fact remains that Alcott chose to write the sweet, family-oriented stuff under her real name and the "sensational" stories under a pseudonym because that was what she wanted and perhaps it's what she felt she had to do.

***

"Vernon Lee was the nom de plume of Violet Paget, a writer of astonishing range and audacity whose published works include historical studies of art and music, dense treatises on aesthetic psychology, acclaimed travel essays, meditations on gardens, pacifist and feminist pamphlets, and supernatural tales" begins a 2018 article in the *Paris Review*. By the late nineteenth century, women were writing more and more under their own names, but Lee was convinced that would never fly for women wanting to write on weightier subjects. "I am sure that no one reads a woman's writing on art, history, or aesthetics with any-thing but unmitigated contempt," she wrote to her mentor, Henrietta Jenkin, in 1878. Reinventing herself as Vernon Lee was an act of innovative artistry in and of itself. Her decision to cast off Violet was a deliberate self-fashioning, and one that was seemingly entwined with her queer identity. In some respects, "Vernon" wasn't a pseudonym at all—even the author's lovers and friends called her by that name. Ana Parejo Vadillo, of Birkbeck, University of London, writes, "That sense of being free from gen-der, free from sex, at a period in which those kinds of categories are very heavily fixed in the minds, was quite important for her."

Vernon Lee was ahead of her time. She was prolific, writing more than forty books in almost every genre, and, together with her lover, Kit Anstruther-Thomson, she developed a theory of

VERNON LEE

psychological aesthetics, writing extensively about how the body physically responds to works of art. She was considered a forward-thinking British Victorian who didn't quite fit into the era, while the new modernists thought her a dusty old Victorian and didn't want her to sit at their lunch table either. Since the 1990s, Lee has been having a bit of a resurgence, and in the twenty-first century many of us tend to value that which the modernists of the early twentieth century perhaps found off-putting: we're okay with folks who don't fit neatly into one camp. Having a hard time boxing Lee in, the world seems to have decided it was cool to forget about her for a while. But don't sleep on Vernon Lee; she is in a category all her own. She deserves our attention.

Pauline Hopkins, who was born in Portland, Maine, in 1859, was the most prolific Black female writer of her time. She is best known for four novels and numerous short stories published between 1900 and 1903. Her most popular work, *Contending Forces: A Romance Illustrative of Negro Life North and South*, was published in Boston in 1900 by the Colored Co-operative Publishing Company. She's also considered one of the original Afrofuturists for having written *Of One Blood* (1902–3), a book of speculative fiction about a utopian African society with advanced technology that many compare to *Black Panther*'s Wakanda. What's equally, if not more, striking was Hopkins's work for the *Colored American Magazine*, which ran from 1900 to 1909 and was the first American monthly publication that covered African American culture. Hopkins was its most prolific

PAULINE HOPKINS

writer, sat on the board as a shareholder, and was editor from 1902 to 1904. Through her writing—which included editorials, fiction, and nonfiction—Hopkins addressed Black history, racial discrimination, economic justice, and women's rights. She was one of her generation's foremost public intellectuals. Hopkins's use of a pseudonym provides a rather thrilling alternative to what we have seen: Hopkins was so prolific in her work for the *Colored American* that she needed to adopt various pseudonyms so that her contributions did not appear to dominate the magazine. It would have been commonplace for one of her articles signed with her real name to sit right next to one of her pieces attributed to a different name altogether.

Hopkins famously clashed with fellow Black intellectual Booker T. Washington. Whereas Washington encouraged

African Americans to stay in the South and had a "compromise" vibe, Hopkins argued that whites should be held accountable for their past involvement in slavery and their ongoing participation in the oppression of Black people. She believed vehemently that the community must demand its civil rights, especially its voting rights. Washington criticized Black Americans for seeking an "impractical" liberal arts education and was seen as someone who did not want to antagonize Southern whites who were against Black suffrage. Hopkins, on the other hand, valued the study of literature and did not wish to impose *any* limits on Black success. While she never bad-mouthed Washington by name, she did criticize key elements of his policy. For all of the above, Hopkins earned the label "agitator" and was ousted as editor of the *Colored American* in 1904, when Washington secretly purchased the magazine.

In an article in *American Periodicals*, Professor Alisha R. Knight tells us that after a failed attempt to start her own magazine, "Hopkins retreated from public life and resumed her work as a stenographer," and that by the time she died in 1930, "her important work as an editor and writer had long been forgotten." Pauline Hopkins deserved better. Her devotion to uplifting Black Americans and specifically Black women should be cherished. How she inserted her politics into everything she wrote is to be revered. Beneath her author photo in *Contending Forces* reads the inscription "Yours for humanity."

To her friends and family, she was Ettie or Etta, but to the rest of the world she was known as Henry Handel Richardson. Born in Melbourne, Ethel Florence Lindesay Richardson was raised in Australia but spent more than fifty-eight years of her life as an expatriate, mostly in England, where she said she never felt "at home." In a 2016 piece for *The Guardian*, her grandniece Angela Neustatter describes how Richardson's identity was revealed in 1929 by the *Daily Telegraph*, comparing her to the unfairly hounded Elena Ferrante.

Richardson, who wrote autobiographical fiction, adopted a male pseudonym to ensure her work would be taken seriously. As told by Germaine Greer, Richardson explained, "There had been much talk in the press about the ease with which a woman's work could be distinguished from a man's; and I wanted to

HENRY HANDEL RICHARDSON

try out the truth of the assertion." Her first novel, *Maurice Guest* (1908), was described by Dame Carmen Callil, famed founder of Virago Press, as "one of the great novels of the 20th century." The acclaimed James Joyce scholar Stuart Gilbert proclaimed, "There is no book previous to *Ulysses* that I have read so often and so often recommended as *Maurice Guest*. To my mind it is the best novel written in the twenty years preceding the war."

After she published several works of fiction to great acclaim, including her masterpiece trilogy, *The Fortunes of Richard Mahony* (1929), the press became determined to uncover the true identity of the reclusive Henry Handel Richardson. According to her grandniece, Richardson herself told of the *Daily Telegraph's* printing a piece "saying my identity as Miss Ettie R had been discovered and disclosed." She never found out who had betrayed her. Being exposed upset her deeply, and she was instantly put off by the requests for interviews that followed. Once, when she was discovered to be on board a cruise ship, the press hounded her so much for an interview that she locked herself in a lavatory until they gave up and went away.

Although she was happily married, she resented the use of her married name, Mrs. J. G. Robertson. According to her longtime secretary and companion, Olga Roncoroni, "In 1935 H. H. was awarded the King George V Silver Jubilee Medal . . . and the accompanying document, headed 'Buckingham Palace,' announced that the award was made to 'Mrs. J. G. Robertson—for her work as an author.' H. H. immediately returned the document, saying that since her work had not been written under her married name, she could not accept the medal under that name. Within a short time, a new document arrived—made out to Henry Handel Richardson.

On this point she was adamant; nothing infuriated her more than a refusal to accept the name under which she had always written." "I've worked more than twenty years to establish my own name," she once said. "Why shouldn't I have it?"

———————

According to the Library of America, *The Street* by Ann Petry remains "unsurpassed for its unblinking portrayal of the realities and challenges of Black, female, working-class life." *The Street* was a literary phenomenon when it was published in 1946. Universally heralded and translated around the world, it was the first book by a Black woman to sell more than a million copies. "To this day," said Coretta Scott King, "few works of fiction have so clearly illuminated the devastating impact of racial injustice."

Petry was born in Old Saybrook, Connecticut, to a pharmacist father and a foot doctor mom. Possessing an innate reticence to being known, she tried her best to keep biographers off her scent. For example, she cited six different birth dates for herself, between 1908 and 1911. Her family was one of only four Black households in her hometown. After she got married, in 1938, she and her husband moved to New York, settling in Harlem. Petry began her literary career working as an editor and a journalist for the *People's Voice* (1942–44), a progressive African American newspaper founded by Adam Clayton Powell Jr.

In 1939, when it came time for the *Afro American* to publish her first short story, a suspense romance called "Marie of the Cabin Club," she used the pseudonym Arnold Petri. In *At Home Inside: A Daughter's Tribute to Ann Petry*, her daughter, Liz Petry, writes, "She gave various reasons for using a pseudonym: that the

ANN PETRY

quality and type work differed from her other stories, that she thought a story by a man was more likely to be published." But, she inevitably concludes, "I never learned her real reasoning."

Petry found sudden celebrity terrifying and experienced fame as a kind of theft. "My soul was no longer my own," she told the *New York Times* in 1992. "I was a black woman at a point in time when being a writer was not usual, and I was besieged. Everyone wanted a part of me." Liz Petry recalls a journal entry her mother wrote during a publicity tour, lamenting, "I feel as though I were a helpless creature impaled on a dissecting table—for public viewing." By 1947, she and her husband had moved back to Connecticut, she stopped giving interviews, and they got an unlisted phone number.

By the time Petry published her megahit *The Street,* she was writing under her own name, but from all accounts it sounds as if she may have wondered why she ever gave up the pseudonym. It's important to note that while she had no appetite for fame, she was not ambivalent about writing. She wanted the largest audience possible to read her work and to receive her messages concerning racism, sexism, and class divide. She just didn't want you to bug her about it.

James Tiptree Jr. exploded onto the science fiction scene in the late 1960s. He was a brilliant and singular talent. In a dazzling 1969 letter, writer and editor Harlan Ellison raved to Tiptree, "You are the single most important new writer in science fiction today. Nobody touches you!" Tiptree was a recluse, a shut-in no one had ever seen or even spoken to on the phone. That's because James Tiptree Jr. was in fact Alice B. Sheldon. It was not made public until 1977 that Tiptree was a woman.

Tiptree was known for being a male author who understood women, a golden example of a male feminist. His lauded novelette *The Women Men Don't See* (1973) involves a woman who begs aliens to take her from earth, no longer wanting to contend with an oppressive male-dominated society. Girl, yes, take me with you! Though Tiptree was a recluse, "he" had many pen pals. One of them, the feminist science fiction writer Joanna Russ, wrote to "him" in 1975 that a professor at a party had "asked me if you were a woman (!) by which I gather he can't recognize a female point of view if it bites him." And according to biographer Julie Phillips, Russ also told him that he had ideas "no woman could even think, or understand, let alone assent to." Huh. Joanna Russ . . . *feminist*, you say?

ALICE B. SHELDON

Alice Sheldon, known to her intimates as Alli, the name she liked best, was a true original, a brilliant mind who did not necessarily *need* Tiptree to flourish. Phillips tells us, "By the time she started writing science fiction she had already been a painter and an air force intelligence officer. . . . She had worked for the CIA. She had earned a Ph.D. in experimental psychology." I mean . . . wow. By the way, Sheldon's writing career did not begin until she was fifty-one years old. So, if you are sitting on a novel, get to it. It's not too late!

In the first in-person interview she ever granted a publication, Sheldon told *Isaac Asimov's Science Fiction Magazine* in 1983, "A male name seemed like good camouflage. I had the feeling that a man would slip by less observed. I've had too many experiences in my life of being the first woman in some damned occupation." What Tiptree gave Sheldon was an opportunity to show all the sides of herself. Tiptree protected her and allowed her the freedom to write about what she knew, like duck hunting, technology, and espionage. She wasn't concerned about being chided for unfeminine writing when as "Tip" she wrote about alien sex or the inner workings of government. Tiptree's writing, chock-full of desire for women, also allowed Sheldon to express her queerness in a safer space than her real life afforded. I simply can't get over this woman and how extraordinary she was. As journalist Charles Platt notes in the *Asimov* profile, "The trouble is, Alice Sheldon's remarkable life is too big for a profile."

Alli's story does not end all tied up and clean with a pretty bow. She lived and she died on her own terms. In 1976, when she was sixty-one years old, she expressed a desire to take her own life, but she was reluctant to leave her elderly husband behind or to kill him. Eventually, she convinced him to make a suicide pact, and at the age of seventy-one, Alli Sheldon took her husband's life and then her own. Their bodies were found on their bed, hand in hand. I'm glad the world knew her, the real her, before she left us. She was no longer the woman men don't see.

I want to leave you with one more name. Joanna Baillie. Who? Exactly. At the beginning of *A Room of One's Own*, Virginia Woolf mentions a woman named Joanna Baillie. Woolf offhandedly refers to the influence Baillie had on the poems of Edgar Allan Poe. I immediately needed to know more.

It turns out Joanna Baillie was compared to Shakespeare during her lifetime. Her prolific oeuvre includes twenty-six plays and numerous volumes of poetry. Even though Baillie "enjoyed fame almost without parallel" during her lifetime, she fell into obscurity soon after her death. Before interest in her work was renewed in the 1980s, biographers and scholars regularly trivialized her work and dismissed her success. Biographer Donald Carswell went so far as to condemn those who celebrated her! Calm down, Donald. Author Catherine B. Burroughs explains, "The tone of hostile bewilderment that persists in Bailliean criticism throughout much of the twentieth century . . . worked to eradicate her significance." She is now recognized for her innovations in character development and for her enormous influence on such writers as William Wordsworth, Lord Byron, and Percy Bysshe Shelley. So, guess what, folks? You can be *compared to Shakespeare* and influence

JOANNA BAILLIE

some of the most acclaimed writers of all time and STILL fall into obscurity and become . . . anonymous. I'm not saying it happened because Baillie was a woman, but I'm not *not* saying it either. Baillie scholar Judith B. Slagle says being written off as a little lady "scribbler" was "a fate similar to that of many other early women writers." Baillie was a giant in her time. She merits remembering.

———————

Virginia Woolf was right. We must write. We must have time and space of our own and we must tell our stories. We cannot judge or blame writers of the past for choosing to be "veiled." It's difficult to imagine a time when the idea of publishing one's work, as a man or as a woman, was considered *unseemly*. Beyond that weird era when sharing your ideas was thought of as embarrassing, it's impossible to comprehend what life was like for women of generations past. It is hard to grasp that there was a time when legends like Brontë and Austen and Shelley were unknown, thriving, in a way, in the shadows. There will always be pen names and myriad reasons for using them. Every writer has the right to decide whether to be known or unknown. That said, I hope we continue to move away from all forms of gender bias in writing, whether it's at the publishing stage, or in marketing, or in deciding who gets reviewed. We've come a long way from Charlotte Brontë and her sisters' fear "that authoresses are liable to be looked on with prejudice," but we are not entirely out of the woods.

———————

IRANIAN WOMEN SNEAKING INTO STADIUMS

With few exceptions, women have been banned from attending stadium football (soccer) matches in Iran since 1981. Yet ardent female football fans have never given up trying various methods to attend games, including disguising themselves as men.

In 2018, a BBC News story went viral about five young Iranian women who had snuck into a football match disguised as men. The story first broke online with photos and videos of the young women being widely shared on both Persian and English social media. Images of the girls decked out in fake beards and ill-fitting wigs, joyously cheering on their team, Persepolis, swept across the internet, until the BBC—and everyone else—finally picked up the story. I was enthralled and I had questions!

Why would it be a crime (or a sin?) for women to be fans of something, joyfully cheering on a team and celebrating camaraderie with other diehards? What's the reasoning here? Before we dig in, a bit of backstory.

The so-called Islamic Revolution of 1979 profoundly changed Iran, most notably for women. I say "so-called" because after consulting with the Iranian American author and professor Melody Moezzi, I understood that a distinction should be made. Moezzi stressed that while the current Iranian regime claims to be an Islamic Republic, it is anything but. The Qur'an explicitly forbids compulsion in religion; it cannot be forced on you. Calling it the "Islamic Revolution" is, therefore, problematic, as so many believe what is being presented and pushed in Iran is *not* Islam at all but a warped interpretation of it. I'm grateful to Moezzi for helping me understand a subject that she says is much too often written about in the West with a lazy pen.

According to Islamic scholar Abdullahi An-Na'im, Iran and a few other countries claim that their laws are based on Shari'a, "a way of life," but in fact, most of those laws are secular. Following the revolution, the new regime instituted what they were calling Shari'a law, which was actually their distorted, politicized interpretation of Islam. As a result, the political and social status of women deteriorated. Many of the rights that Iranian women had gained before the revolution were systematically abolished through legislation. But Iran is also a conundrum of a country with several polarities. For instance, female education and literacy rates have increased dramatically since 1979, while women's rights have been curtailed.

One area that swiftly came under scrutiny postrevolution was the way women dressed and wore their hair. The pro-Western Reza Shah Pahlavi of the 1930s had banned veils and headscarves and encouraged his people to adopt European dress. It was his policy to increase women's participation in society as a way of modernizing the country. That sounds like WOOHOO, the old Shah was pro-women and wanted equality and everything must've been hunky-dory, right? Sadly, no. Most of the laws he enacted were only superficial and didn't deviate much from the conservative norms of the past. And, get this, to enforce the no-headscarves decree, the Shah ordered police to go around and physically remove the veil from any woman who wore it in public. Women were beaten, their headscarves ripped from their bodies. Call me crazy, but physically assaulting a woman and forcing her to dress a certain way is a funny way to communicate that she is free and that your country is becoming "modernized." Also, how different is "YOU MUST WEAR THIS OR WE WILL PUNCH YOU" from "YOU MUST NEVER WEAR THIS OR WE WILL PUNCH YOU"?

Needless to say, That Old Shah's ruthless modes of enforcement undermined any progress he was trying to make. His own son, That Other Shah, Mohammed Reza Pahlavi, wrote in his memoir *Mission for My Country*, "Reza Shah never advocated a complete break with the past, for he always assumed that girls could find their best fulfillment in marriage. . . . But he was convinced that a girl could be a better wife and mother, as well as a better citizen, if she received an education." That makes me think of some of the advice doled out to American women in the 1950s and '60s (and '70s and '80s and '90s): "Go to college so you can get your M.R.S. degree."

While Mohammed Reza's reign (1941–79) was characterized by corruption and internal conflict, the photos you see of women in Iran before the revolution (when he was overthrown) are remarkable: women studying alongside men at university, wearing Western clothing, including miniskirts and jewelry, and full faces of makeup. You see images of women and men congregating together at picnics, at a hair salon, dancing at a nightclub. And both men and women were allowed into stadiums to watch sporting events.

As an aside, I'd be remiss to mention the 1979 revolution without also mentioning the CIA- and MI5-backed coup of 1953, in which the Brits and the Yanks got their knickers in a knot because democratically elected prime minister Mossadegh was trying to nationalize oil. As Moezzi puts it, "1979 wouldn't have happened if the US hadn't gotten so mad when Mossadegh did that—God forbid Iranians could benefit from their own natural resources." When it started, the revolution was about freeing Iran from the shackles of colonialism. What ended up happening to the people of Iran after the revolution was *not* what they had signed up for.

After the revolution, public schools were desecularized. Women who were previously thriving in engineering programs were suddenly banned because it was deemed "a male industry." Abortion, which was legalized in Iran in 1977, was quickly criminalized again after Ayatollah Ruhollah Khomeini took power. (In 2005, it became legal in certain "medically necessary" circumstances.) And in the early 1980s, the new regime imposed a mandatory dress code that required all women to wear the hijab.

Okay, so why is it a crime for a woman to cheer for her favorite sports team in public? Well, apparently it isn't actually a crime at all, but that does not stop Iranian officials from refusing women entry, sometimes detaining those who try to enter, and sometimes even prosecuting them. It's infuriating for obvious reasons, but because there is no actual, official ban or crime, it's also deeply unsettling that the line is free to keep being moved in terms of how one official or another might choose to handle a woman who attempts to enter a sports stadium.

Sometimes the authorities only go so far as to contact the parents of the young women as punishment, but some women are also full-on arrested for attending games. In 2014, authorities arrested the Iranian British woman Ghoncheh Ghavami along with some twenty others when they tried attending a World League volleyball match. They were released, but Ghavami was rearrested and charged with "propaganda against the state." She was imprisoned and, according to Human Rights Watch, kept in solitary confinement for nearly five months. In March 2018, about a month before the viral story of the five disguised women at the Persepolis match, thirty-five women were detained for trying to attend a game. These ever-fluctuating punishments make it all the more astounding that women will risk so much to disguise their way into a sporting event in their questionable wigs, YouTube tutorial makeup, and heaps and heaps of GUTS. It's so fucking brave. It's essential for me to point out that the main thing I have learned in my research is that Iranian women are unmitigated BADASSES. They are *wildly* defiant. It's awe inspiring.

In June 2018, it was announced that *some* women would be permitted to enter Tehran's Azadi Stadium to watch the World Cup match between Iran and Spain. Women lined up outside with their tickets, vibrating with excitement. No fake beards necessary! But they were soon informed that they would not be admitted, that the plan had been canceled due to "infrastructure issues." (There's that sneaky moving line again!) Fans began to chant in protest, and some staged a sit-in, refusing to leave until they were let in.

According to a BBC News report, videos of the protests circulated on social media and the hashtag #Azadi_cancellation (in Persian) trended on Twitter. After a last-minute special-order flip-flop by the interior minister, Abdolreza Rahmani Fazli, fans were finally admitted before kickoff. All this hubbub and hand-wringing because women wanted to WATCH SPORTS. Yeesh! In the end, a few hundred female fans, in a stadium with a capacity of almost eighty thousand, were allowed in to watch the match—the first time that had happened on that scale in about forty years.

While there are many die-hard female football fans in Iran, some of the women who attended that Iran-Spain game didn't even care much for the sport. According to the photojournalist Forough Alaei, "They just came, they said, to enter a stadium once in their lives," one of them telling her, "she was so happy to see inside a stadium before she died."

Letting a few hundred women into the stadium one time was not the sea change Iranian women were looking for. Far from it. Women were still being turned away from matches, still sporting disguises, and still defiantly showing up at the stadium having no idea what might happen to them if their identities were discovered. Because that sneaky line kept moving, they wouldn't know if it would be a slap on the wrist or worse.

And sometimes it is much, much worse. A story we hear less about—perhaps because it is just too horrific to even think about—is of twenty-nine-year-old Sahar Khodayari, who faced a six-month prison sentence for trying to enter a football stadium disguised as a man in March 2019. In response, and to raise awareness about the ban, Khodayari doused herself with gasoline and set herself on fire in front of the Islamic Revolutionary Court of Tehran. She died from her injuries a week later.

Khodayari's gruesome death renewed and escalated the debate about barring Iranian women from attending sporting matches. A letter from FIFA (the international governing body of football/soccer) to the Islamic Republic insisted that Iranian women be allowed to enter all football stadiums across the country to watch men's matches. Within weeks, the president of FIFA said Iranian authorities had assured him that women would be allowed to attend international matches, beginning with the World Cup qualifier against Cambodia in October 2019. Nevertheless, only approximately 3,500 women were permitted to enter the Azadi for that match. Photos in the *New York Times* show the women segregated behind metal fencing, with a buffer of empty sections keeping them far away and separate from the men.

Tehran's Azadi Stadium (*azadi* means "freedom" in Persian, by the way) has an official capacity of about 78,000. But in 1998 all records were broken when the attendance hit 128,000 for a FIFA World Cup qualifying match against Australia. Officials seemingly had to break some rules for such a thing to happen, to accommodate all those adoring (male) fans, filling the stadium beyond what anyone thought it could hold. Breaking rules to break records . . . to make sure everyone had an opportunity to show their love of the game.

Sometimes rules are meant to be broken.

A video that went viral on Twitter in 2020 shows a woman in Iran riding a bicycle without the traditional hijab. The wind is blowing her hair and she triumphantly raises her right arm, both in an act of defiance and seemingly waving at shocked onlookers. She was arrested. "A person who had recently violated norms and insulted the Islamic veil in this region has been arrested," Mojtaba Raei, the governor of Najafabad, told the Islamic Republic News Agency (IRNA). Several other videos of unveiled women, joyfully and defiantly riding their bikes, soon began cropping up on social media. These women were apparently committing *two* crimes. In 2016, Ayatollah Ali Khamenei explicitly banned women from riding a bike in public, but it was not strictly enforced. As of 2019, however, more and more officials seem to be adhering to the fatwa, and the regime considers it *haram* for a woman to ride a bike in public, whether she is veiled or not.

Also in 2020, an online campaign and hashtag caught on when Iranian women began filming their harassers with their camera phones and uploading the footage to social media. The hashtag, going strong to this day, is #MyCameraIsMyWeapon. In the countless videos, women document men accosting them in public for not wearing a hijab. When the women pull out their cameras and begin filming, most of the men slink off or drive away. Some of the videos begin with men sexually harassing an unveiled woman, but when the harasser realizes he's being filmed, his tune changes immediately to giving her a finger-wagging sermon about her uncovered head. Just like the women who sneak into stadiums disguised as men, what these women are doing is unfathomably brave. I stand with the women of Iran and hope that one day they can do whatever they want and wear what they want, including the hijab, and not be subjected to constant policing.

Terrified by what had just happened, Switzer thought about stopping. She was shocked by the ruckus that *she* had caused, all because she wanted to run a goddamn marathon. Her fears, however, soon morphed into fierce determination. She knew she had to finish the race, even if it meant finishing on her hands and knees. It became crystal clear to her: No one thinks I can do it. And the weight of the moment, of being the first official female entrant in the Boston Marathon . . . she knew exactly what so many other female firsts know: If she didn't finish, it wouldn't mean that Kathrine Switzer couldn't finish a marathon, it would mean that NO WOMAN could. Having all of that resting on her shoulders in that moment LIT. HER. UP.

After Switzer finished the race in her blood-soaked shoes, with a running time of four hours and twenty minutes, she was deemed illegitimate. Semple had called the Amateur Athletic Union (AAU), the organization that governed amateur competitive sports in the United States, and had Switzer disqualified and expelled for these offenses: 1. running with men; 2. running more than 1½ miles (the longest distance allowed for women); 3. fraudulently entering the marathon (as K. V. Switzer); and 4. running without a chaperone. DEAR LORD.

The AAU had a lot of power. It organized every major track-and-field event and marathon, and decided who was worthy of competing in other countries and who would go to the Olympics. It ruled with an iron fist. No amateur athlete wanted to piss off the AAU for fear it could hamper their chances of making it to the Olympics. So even if some male runners disagreed with the AAU's stance on female athletes, they often didn't show support publicly.

If you were banned from the AAU, like Switzer, you weren't allowed to compete at all, anywhere—officially, that is. Even though Switzer was banned from the AAU and was not officially allowed to run, race directors across the United States invited her to participate unofficially. The

CATHAY WILLIAMS

Cathay Williams was the first and only female Buffalo Soldier and the only documented Black woman to serve in the United States Army in the nineteenth century. And she did so disguised as a man. Cathay Williams was born into slavery in Independence, Missouri, sometime between 1844 and 1850. Her father was a free Black man, and her mother was enslaved, making her legal status that of an enslaved person. Cathay became a "house girl" with her mother on the Johnson plantation, on the outskirts of Jefferson City. A vehemently contested border state, Missouri was a hotbed of guerrilla activity during the Civil War. Populated by both Union

and Confederate sympathizers, it was like the North and the South all in one. It was tense! Missouri was like when you go home for Thanksgiving and your Confederate flag–loving uncle is at the head of the table talking about immigration . . . except all the time, every day.

At the start of the Civil War, Missouri governor Claiborne Fox Jackson, who was pro-slavery and totally into the Confederacy and who also sounds like he coulda been a big racist cartoon bird on television, defiantly rejected Lincoln's request for troops because he was like "fuck the Union" and instead assembled a volunteer militia with the covert intention of getting Missouri to join the Confederacy. In June 1861, Union general Nathaniel Lyon was like "I don't think so, bro" as his men surrounded and captured the militia, successfully occupying the state capital, Jefferson City. A provisional military government was put in place to help secure Missouri for the Union. As an aside, I will say that I once thought that everyone who fought for the Union was an abolitionist and basically super against the practice of human beings owning other human beings. Turns out: nope! Nathaniel Lyon is a perfect example. Lyon *was* anti-slavery, but he was adamantly *not* an abolitionist. He opposed slavery because he believed that enslaved labor created unwanted competition for white laborers, NOT because it was, like, an atrocity. Several sources identify Lyon as a passionate abolitionist, which he was not, so don't give him too much credit, because it's not so black and white . . . so to speak.

With the Union staking their claim to Missouri in 1861, Black people like Cathay were suddenly no longer slaves, but they were not entirely free either. They were deemed "contraband," or "captured enemy property," and they were pretty much forced to serve in the Union Army in support roles, such as cooks, laundresses, and nurses.

Years later, in an 1876 interview with the *St. Louis Daily Times*, Cathay recalled that when the soldiers "came to Jefferson City they took me and other colored folks with them to Little Rock. Colonel Benton of the 13th army corps was the officer that carried us off. I did not want to go. He wanted me to cook for the officers but I had always been a house girl and did not know how to cook. I learned to cook after going to Little Rock."

At this point, Cathay would have been a teenager, and it's unclear if she got to stay with her mother or if they were separated. Being born into slavery is horrific enough, but being removed from your mother as you're being dragged off to work for the army is unfathomable. She was so young.

She was assigned the role of cook and washerwoman, which meant she accompanied the infantry all over the country. During these travels under General Philip Sheridan, Williams witnessed the Red River Campaign, the Battle of Pea Ridge, and Sheridan's raids in the Shenandoah Valley.

When the war ended in 1865, Cathay was suddenly a free woman. Postwar job opportunities for newly freed African Americans—especially African American women— were extremely limited. Black women could get work as washerwomen or servants or, if lucky, the highest paid and highest status position: cook. Many Black men felt they had little choice but to turn to military service to gain employment stability. Cathay discovered that being a soldier paid even more than a cook. For this reason, and perhaps because she was already familiar with army customs and culture, she boldly decided to disguise herself as a man and enlist in the United States Army! The history of African American names is a heartbreaking one, given that surnames were often those of the enslavers, but now Cathay was taking charge of her life and choosing her own name, and she chose William Cathay.

At the time of her enlistment on November 15, 1866, William Cathay was assigned to the Thirty-Eighth US Infantry, which was officially established in August 1866 as a designated, segregated African American unit, one of the legendary Buffalo Soldier regiments. Cathay identified herself as five foot nine and twenty-two years old, though it was later discovered that she had probably upped her age and may have only been sixteen or seventeen.

According to Cathay, "Only two persons, a cousin and a particular friend, members of the regiment, knew that I was a woman. They never 'blowed' on me. They were partly the cause of my joining the army. Another reason was I wanted to make my own living and not be dependent on relations or friends. . . . I was a good soldier."

The Thirty-Eighth Infantry was a company of foot soldiers. They marched. Everywhere. Cavalry meant you were on horseback and infantry meant that you were on foot. Even though Cathay suffered a bout of smallpox and was in and out of hospitals with various ailments throughout her military career, she marched hundreds upon hundreds of arduous miles with her company. One such march was Fort Union to Fort Bayard in New Mexico Territory . . . that's four hundred miles, people! And that was just ONE of their treks.

The fact that upward of five hospital visits throughout her military career failed to reveal that Cathay was a woman brings into question the caliber of medical care available to Black soldiers, even by mid-nineteenth-century standards. Eventually Cathay's various ailments took a toll on her, and it is not entirely clear whether she outed herself as a woman to one of the army surgeons or whether a physician finally discovered her identity during an exam. After two years of service in the Thirty-Eighth, her commanding officer, Captain Charles E. Clarke, discharged William Cathay on October 14, 1868. The captain's statement read that Cathay had been under his command since May 20, 1867, "and has been since feeble both physically and mentally, and much of the time quite unfit for duty. The origin of his infirmities is unknown to me."

Was she as unfit for service as her discharge certificate states? Or was it exaggerated because they had discovered she was a woman and needed to tout these deficiencies as the reason for her dismissal? There is no mention in William Cathay's discharge about him being a woman, but we know they knew. Yes, she suffered her ailments, but Captain Clarke's emphasis on how "feeble both physically and mentally" William was, is a bit dubious. Cathay was certainly clever enough to conceal herself and pass as a male foot soldier for two years, which speaks to both her fitness and mental acuity. The guy sounds like he had a bug up his butt because he didn't realize one of his privates was a she.

After leaving the army, Cathay went back to living as a woman, working as a cook and a laundress in New Mexico Territory and then in Colorado. A 2009 profile in the *Pueblo Chieftain* states that she spent time living and working in Pueblo, Colorado, while her mother, a woman they identify as Martha Williams, was working at a local orphanage; if accurate, it is bolstering to know that mother and daughter were reunited. When a reporter from the *St. Louis Daily Times* came calling in 1875–76 to do his profile on Cathay, she was living in Trinidad, Colorado. In September 1891, records show that a medical doctor employed by the Pension Bureau examined her, as she was seeking a disability pension. The documentation from this exam is incomplete and incongruous. They claim either that her disability didn't exist or that it existed prior to her enlistment. If that were true, why would she have been permitted to enlist? Hmmm . . . citing a preexisting condition to deny someone medical care? In the United States? As the great David Byrne once said, "Same as it ever was. Same as it ever was."

One can't help but think about the long lonnnnng history of not taking Black women's ailments seriously. Not to mention the very real possibility that they were punishing a Black woman for having fooled them in the first place. The Pension Bureau rejected her claim, stating that she did not have a disability. When you think of all the marching Cathay had to do in the Thirty-Eighth and all the times she was in and out of the hospital during her army service, not to mention everything she contributed to the Union

Army when she was forced to serve during the Civil War . . . I'm sorry, but they did her dirty. Absolute crap.

When Cathay Williams enlisted in the army as a man, she was not trying to make a point, she was not aiming to be a pioneer. She was simply trying to LIVE. To feel as free and independent and self-sufficient as she could, attempting to move beyond her earlier life, which began in bondage and servitude. It is fair to say that Cathay was victorious, despite the maladies, hardship, and racism she faced. She occupies a significant place in the history of African American women in the military. Williams exemplifies the myriad ways Black women have found to survive treacherous periods in history. Her career as a soldier was not filled with decorations and medals, but her courage, determination, and self-actualization remain awe inspiring. The exact date of Cathay's death is unknown, but it is assumed she died in Trinidad, Colorado, in 1893. A bronze bust memorial was dedicated to her in 2016 at the Richard Allen Cultural Center and Museum in Leavenworth, Kansas.

CATALINA DE ERAUSO

Catalina de Erauso, the daughter of a prominent noble family, was born in Donostia-San Sebastián, in the Basque region of Spain, in 1585 or 1592, depending on whether you consult her baptism certificate or her memoir. Just like every other noble-born girl, Catalina was sent off to a convent when she was four years old for her education-slash-taming. Her family eventually concluded that she was too rebellious and caustic to land herself a husband, so they offered her up to the most forgiving man they could think of: God. (It was a long time ago, so they didn't know God was a nonbinary femme yet.) As it turns out, God had other plans. On the eve of taking her vows, fifteen-year-old Catalina escaped the convent, cut off her hair, fashioned boy's clothes from her habit (*Project Runway* could never), and set out to lead the most adventurous, and often quite problematic, life one could imagine. Over the next twenty years, Catalina de Erauso was a shop boy, sailed to South America with conquistadores, was a soldier of fortune in a brutal tour to Chile, participated in Spanish colonization, almost perished when the Dutch pummeled her ship in Lima, dueled, gambled, pillaged, and murdered aplenty.

By all accounts, she was not what you might call "a good person." Criminal activity, a hot temper, and violence seemed to be Catalina's MO. She was the very definition of an anti heroine. Once, at the theater, she became enraged and slashed a dude's face for blocking her view when he sat in front of her while wearing a tall hat! While I do not condone that behavior, I did get into an argument with a woman who brought a fake service dog to the Off-Broadway run of *The Humans* so . . . I understand it? As we established with the witch-pricker, not everyone in this book is going to be a goodly person. Catalina went her own way. She was an opportunistic adventurer who defied all "feminine" expectations, made decisions by and for herself, and became infamous.

Erauso's father, Captain Miguel de Erauso, was a high-ranking military commander under Philip II of Spain. Noble though she was, the world Catalina was born into offered her two options: nun or wife. Ironically, being a nun would have offered more autonomy and self-actualization. You had the luxury of time, books to read, thoughts to have, not to mention a community of female friends to commiserate with about your monthly "courses," when women's bodies needed to get rid of their surplus blood because if they didn't they might drown. Yep!

After Catalina escaped the convent, she stayed close to home for the first couple of years. She took odd jobs here and there, and even had some close-call run-ins with her family, who didn't even recognize her. According to her *autobiografía*, her life was one adventure, dispute, or sticky situation after another. That no doubt was deliberate, considering that she wrote the book when the picaresque novel (a genre of prose fiction that depicts the adventures of a roguish but appealing hero) was exceedingly popular. Of course, scholars question how much of her memoir is fiction, which is an all-too-common theme: questioning adventurous women who had the audacity to allow their story to be shared. But given that the picaresque novel *was* all the rage, it certainly is possible, if not likely, that she did some "punch up" to her story. Catalina, who went by various aliases (Pedro de Orive, Francisco de Loyola, Alonso Díaz Ramirez de Guzmán, and Antonio de Erauso), wasn't *only* about the marauding and the pilfering. She lost one of the less murderous jobs she had, that of shop boy, because she was frolicking with the shopkeeper's daughter, detailed in this titillating passage from her book: "One day when she and I were in the front parlour, and I had my head in the folds of her skirt and she was combing my hair while I ran my hand up and down between her legs, Diego de Solarte happened to pass by the window, and spied us through the grate." Yowza.

Catalina certainly was a gender-nonconforming individual. In her auto-biography, she uses masculine and feminine pronouns interchangeably, but she does identify herself at the outset as a woman telling her tale. What's most compelling is that more than her gender or sexual identity, her major defining identity, which she emphasizes again and again, is her Basque heritage.

Basques proudly distinguish themselves from other Spaniards and are known for their solidarity. The Basque ethnic group comes from a region of southwest France and northwest Spain known to outsiders as Basque and to Basque people as Euskal Herria. "Euskal" refers to Euskara, the Basque language, which is linguistically distinct from French, Spanish, or any other language. In Catalina's time there was a strong "us against them" mentality among her people. Catalina used her Basque identity again and again to get preferential treatment, to escape legal consequences, to obtain work or safe passage to the Americas . . . you name it. Her ethnic origins, her Basque identity, and how she *used* this identity went hand in hand with her presenting and living as a man . . . both provided her access, privilege, and, indeed, survival.

Catalina was never suspected to be female until one day, after yet another scrap, she found herself badly wounded, and just as she had done many times before, she sought refuge in a church, seeking the help of a bishop. Here, seemingly on the brink of death, and maybe feeling a need to pull out ALL the stops to try to save her life, she confessed to him:

> *Your Grace, all of this that I have told you . . . in truth, it is not so. The truth is this: that I am a woman, that I was born in such and such a place, the daughter of this man and this woman, that at a certain age I was placed in a convent*

with a certain aunt; that I was raised there and took the veil and became a nov-
ice, and that when I was about to profess my final vows, I left the convent for
such and such a reason, went to such and such a place, undressed myself, dressed
myself up again, cut my hair, traveled here and there, embarked, disembarked,
hustled, killed, maimed, wreaked havoc, and roamed about until coming to a
stop in this very instant, at the feet of Your Eminence.

After Catalina's big disclosure she became a legit, no-joke CELEBRITY, which is simply jaw-dropping. It must be reiterated: this time in history was not permissive! Ever hear of the Spanish Inquisition? Admittedly, most of my knowledge about the Inquisition comes from Mel Brooks's *History of the World, Part I*, but the point was made: *lots* of torture. Nevertheless, Catalina was not executed or even shunned when her transgressions became public. She became . . . popular. First, she spent three years in a Peruvian convent while her story was investigated; they needed all that time to determine if she had taken her final vows at that first convent as a girl . . . clearly the wi-fi was *really* slow back then. If she *had* taken her vows, they would send her back there to live out the rest of her days because *a deal's a deal*. It was, however, established that she had *not* taken her final vows, and she was released and returned to Spain.

During the three years she was detained, Catalina was also subjected to a physical examination and found to be *virgo intacta*—a virgin. This point is important because her virginal status was her golden ticket in the eyes of the Church. It is what made everything about her acceptable.

In 1625, she boldly petitioned the Spanish king for a pension, even though she was never a formal member of the military, and she was successful in her application! It was also about this time that she wrote (or dictated) her autobiography. Then she traveled to Rome and MET THE POPE. She told Pope Urban VIII her story, that she was born a woman, that she had managed to keep her virginity all this time (definitely his favorite part), and, as she tells it, he "graciously gave me leave to pursue my life in men's clothing" but with one caveat: He strongly encouraged her not to kill any more people.

It is utterly baffling that the Spanish state not only punished homosexuality with death, but documentation shows that female cross-dressing was banned *several* times—in 1600, 1608, 1615, and 1641. All those dates coincide with Erauso's life. So, why did Catalina not only escape punishment but find herself lauded?

The author and professor Marjorie Garber posits a sort of loophole: "That she was commended by the pope for this impenetrability suggests that her intact hymen somehow reconciles her lifestyle and her biological sex. An unpenetrated woman may behave like a man; therefore, an unpenetrated woman is not really a woman."

Erauso is a rather titillating enigma. She utilized and performed the most aggressive masc symbols of heteropatriarchal Western imperialism and conquest throughout her narrative while she performed the transgressive act of disguising herself as a man to do so. She participated in rigid gender norms while simultaneously challenging them!

In 1635, befitting an enigma, Catalina disappeared from a ship during a tempestuous storm. Some say that she lived another fifteen years in the small Mexican village of Cotaxtla, where she died in her late fifties. No matter how she met her end, Erauso boldly defied society and the path laid out for her. She had as many flaws as enemies as fans. She chose her life, one that was full of adventures spanning two continents, rather than allowing others to choose. We may not be able to love or even like Catalina, but one can admire her daring—bolting from a nunnery into the rather treacherous world of colonial Latin America and not only surviving that shit but attaining legendary status.

TARPÉ MILLS

In 1938, the release of Action Comics #1 changed the world forever when it introduced America to a fella by the name of Superman, and the superhero genre was born. That was the beginning of what is known as the Golden Age of comics. Three years later, in April 1941, another game changer showed up: the first female superhero. Nope, not Wonder Woman—she would arrive eight months later in her star-spangled blue skirt (the high-waisted control-top briefs would come later). No, the FIRST female superhero was Miss Fury, created, written, and drawn by Tarpé Mills, who *also* happened to be a woman.

June Tarpé Mills was born in Brooklyn in 1912 or 1918, depending on the source. She was raised by a single mother, a widowed working woman who raised June and the children of June's deceased sister. Mills worked as a model to help support her family and then to put herself through

New York's prestigious Pratt Institute, where she studied fashion illustration. Side note: Pratt Institute, founded in 1887, was one of the first colleges in the country open to all people, regardless of gender, race, or class.

After a brief stint as a fashion illustrator, Mills started her comics career with her first comic, *Daredevil Barry Finn*, published in 1938 by Centaur Publications. As cartoonist and historian Trina Robbins writes, "From the beginning, Mills signed her comics with her sexually ambiguous middle name, a French-sounding version of her Irish grandmother's maiden name, Tarpey." Mills later told the *New York Post*, "It would have been a major let-down to the kids if they found out that the author of such virile and awesome characters was a gal."

Mills's career was going swimmingly, with her work regularly appearing in *Amazing Mystery Funnies*, *Reg'lar Fellers Heroic Comics*, and *Target Comics*, as she crafted such stand-out characters as the Catman and the Purple Zombie. However, the more coveted job in comics back then was the steady and reliable work of a weekly strip in a newspaper. This prestigious gig was not easy to come by, but in 1941 Tarpé Mills's tremendous artistic talent and glamorous flair led her to sign a contract with the Bell syndicate to begin writing her game-changing Sunday strip *The Black Fury* (which soon became *Miss Fury*), featuring the first major female superhero ever.

With *Fury*, Tarpé Mills introduced the world to smart and seductive socialite Marla Drake, whose origin story as Miss Fury slyly thumbs its nose at the traditionally macho conventions of the superhero genre. Marla finds out that she and her friend Carol are wearing identical gowns to a masquerade ball. So, instead, she dons a skintight black leopard suit that had been given to her by her uncle and that once belonged to an African witch doctor. On her way to the soirée, Marla accidentally stumbles into vigilantism when she helps recapture an escaped murderer, disarming him using her suit's claws, her quick thinking, and a puff of powder blown from her compact. And just like that, Miss Fury was born. Hey, I know it's not being bitten by a radioactive spider . . . it's *better*.

In November 1941, seven months after the strip began, *The Black Fury* was renamed *Miss Fury*. Even leading Tarpé Mills expert Trina Robbins doesn't know why. It's possible the change was made to really hit home that this superhero was a female, the likes of whom had never been seen before. The strip also reflected what was happening in the American workforce: women taking on roles and jobs previously reserved for the men who were now away, serving overseas. Fittingly, instead of random bad guys and gangsters, the villains in *Miss Fury* soon became colorful, wild, and weird Nazis, including archnemesis Erica von Kampf (yes, my friends, *Kampf*), a sexy spy who concealed a swastika-branded forehead beneath her bangs.

Miss Fury's popularity exploded, and there was no way for Mills to continue being an anonymous creator who hid behind an idiosyncratic, gender-neutral name. When the truth was discovered, newspapers hopped on the red-hot story that Tarpé Mills was in fact a dame! The *Fury* strip had been running for about a year when the *New York Post* announced on April 6, 1942: "Meet the Real Miss Fury—It's All Done with Mirrors." Tarpé Mills not only created the first female superhero and not only was she herself a woman, but she based the look and style of her glamorous protagonist on herself. Yes, Marla/Miss Fury LOOKED like Mills. A woman in 1941 creating a female superhero was groundbreaking enough; the fact that said superhero was made in her own image is stunning. It's no wonder the newspapers all viewed Mills as fabulous World War II–era fodder. Soon Mills was being featured in *Time* magazine and the *Miami Daily Herald*. According to the Tarpé Mills website, images of Miss Fury in her black catsuit went on to adorn the nose of "no less than four B17 and B24 bombers, serving in the European and South Pacific theatres." Tarpé Mills and her creation were a sensation.

While there has been progress, comics have far too often featured female characters who existed for the sole purpose of being saved by the male protagonist, or, an even worse fate, they were "fridged," a contemporary term that refers to the slaying of a female character to intensify the hero's motivation and move his story forward, making her a plot device rather than a fully realized character. The term, coined by legendary comic book writer Gail Simone, who also coined "Women in Refrigerators," was inspired by an issue of *Green Lantern*, in which Kyle Rayner, the title hero, comes home to find that his girlfriend, Alexandra DeWitt, has been killed and stuffed in the refrigerator.

There would be no "fridging" in Tarpé Mills's work. She had a very different idea about what female comic characters could and should be: complex, capable women who didn't need superpowers *or* a man to get shit done. In Mills's slyly subversive world, it was the men who often needed saving and who were portrayed as lovesick, with sappy and tortured thought balloons above their heads. Even in *Wonder Woman*, which was created by the self-proclaimed feminist William Moulton Marston, the superheroine pines over love interest Steve Trevor. The author even goes so far as to depict Diana Prince as being jealous of her own alter ego because Steve fancies Wonder Woman more. Tarpé Mills was downright radical in her portrayal of Marla Drake as someone who had more than one love interest and who never pined over men. It is the men who pine in *Miss Fury*.

Another striking thing about *Miss Fury* is that Marla Drake is sharp and skillful even when she is not in the black catsuit. The comic consistently highlights Marla's depth of ability, like showing her on a fishing trip, angling effortlessly before she runs off to battle evil. Even her physical conquests are portrayed as being possible because of her wits. Unlike Diana Prince, Marla Drake does not have superpowers, yet she is more self-reliant and independent than her Amazonian peer. Nor is she a super genius who achieves feats outside the realm of possibility to readers. She is a viable and relatable hero who is simply courageous and competent and who happens to be a grade-A hottie. One of Tarpé Mills's unparalleled contributions to comics was how she added a level of hyper detail and accuracy to her characters' wardrobe, her background in fashion illustration serving her

well. It was the first time in comics that such attention was given to fashion. Previously, characters, mostly drawn by men, appeared in simple blue suits or basic red dresses, but as the *Los Angeles Review of Books* puts it, "*Miss Fury*, by contrast, is midcentury clothes porn."

The comic won over both men and women. There was action *and* intrigue *and* sexiness *and* feminism *and* depth of character *and* fashion and WOW. Come for the ten-panel catfight between Miss Fury and hot Nazi Erica von Kampf, wrestling on a rooftop in gauzy lingerie, stay for the fashion, female empowerment, and making men the lovelorn puppies. Something for everyone!

Halfway through the series, Marla, dissatisfied with only fighting bad guys, gets a job, and—shockingly, for the times—adopts the abandoned baby of her chief adversary, Erica, becoming a single mother. Tarpé Mills not only gave her readers a female character who defied all societal expectations and gender norms, she also gave the world the first depiction of a superhero who was a mom when positively portraying a single mother, one who had agency, was simply unheard of.

After the war, American women lost their jobs to returning servicemen (because duh, *you've had your fun being strong and capable but get out of the way, the men are back*), and the energy began to shift around how women should be portrayed in comics. One wouldn't think comics would be so policed, but in conservative postwar America, the daddies—I mean men— in charge thought that comics were corrupting young minds and even began linking juvenile delinquency to the increasing number of unconventional comic-book heroines. By 1954, the Comics Code Authority was formed. To meet code approval, a comic couldn't be lurid or excessively violent, and women were to be portrayed in traditional gender roles. It was in this climate that *Miss Fury*'s run came to an end. Couldn't even let us have make-believe.

It's such a shame that while *Wonder Woman* flourished, *Miss Fury* faded from memory and has little to no legacy. It ran for more than a decade, from 1941 to 1952, and was syndicated in one hundred different newspapers at the height of its wartime fame. Timely Comics (now Marvel) obtained the rights to reprint the strips in comic-book form and ran it as a series from 1942 to 1946, selling a million copies an issue.

Even though Miss Fury and Tarpé Mills are both feminist icons, there is no biography about Mills's life, which is utterly disappointing and why much of this chapter is about Miss Fury, not Ms. Mills. One can barely find the compilation volumes of *Miss Fury* (published by IDW in 2011 and 2013), as they are out of print. If Timely reprinted the strips in the 1940s and Timely has since become Marvel, why isn't Marvel all over the *Miss Fury* legacy and resurgence? WHERE'S THE *MISS FURY* MOVIE?

In 2019, Mills's work and legacy were finally recognized with her induction into the Eisner Awards Hall of Fame at Comic-Con in San Diego. There she resides—finally—where she belongs, alongside the other, mostly male, creators of the Golden Age. In the beginning, Mills may have felt compelled to hide her gender, but she never hid her convictions about female empowerment and self-sufficiency in her work. She also had a style no one could touch. Now, if you'll excuse me, I need to go daydream about which actress should star in the film.

PILI HUSSEIN

In Tanzania, Pili Hussein dreamed of making her fortune prospecting for precious tanzanite, said to be a thousand times rarer than diamonds. But in her culture, a woman would never be permitted down in the mines, so, in the 1980s she disguised herself as a man and fooled everyone for a decade, covertly becoming Tanzania's first female miner.

Pili came from a large family. Pili's dad had six wives and thirty-eight children. Hey, all of you who were the ignored youngest of six . . . imagine being the youngest of *thirty-eight*! In her youth, Pili's dad often treated her just like one of her brothers and gave her livestock to tend to, which she really didn't care for. She also didn't care much for being married off to someone who turned out to be an abusive husband. So, at the age of

thirty-one, Pili looked around—at the dowry culture, the violent dipshit she was married to, the prison that was becoming her home—and said, *Fuck this, I'm worth more than twelve goats, a milking cow, and a water pump* and ran away to begin a new life. The fortitude!

Ambitious and in search of work, Pili found her way to Mererani, in the foothills of Africa's highest mountain, Kilimanjaro—the only place in the world to mine for tanzanite, a rare, violet-blue gemstone. Tanzanite is a fairly new gem, given its relatively recent discovery in 1967. Besides being one thousand times rarer than diamonds, it is said to generate calmness and compassion and, wouldn't you know it, it's believed to support the starting of a new life. How fitting!

Okay, so there's Pili hanging out in Mererani, knowing she's in precious tanzanite country with opportunities all around her, except the opportunities were only open to men. But that didn't stop determined and tenacious Pili. As she told the BBC, "Women were not allowed in the mining area, so I entered bravely like a man, like a strong person. You take big trousers, you cut them into shorts and you appear like a man. That's what I did." In 1988, Pili disguised herself, adopted a brave, confident swagger, and started going by the nickname Mjomba Hussein (Uncle Hussein). Gender roles be damned, she became a miner! She worked down in the hot, cramped mines, some of which extended a third of a mile underground, for ten to twelve hours a day, hell-bent on finding tanzanite and a new and better life for herself.

Pili elaborates, "I was a leader, I could go six hundred metres under, into the mine. I would do this more bravely than many other men. I was very strong and I was able to deliver what men would expect another man could do. I would do this bravely, so they could not really recognize that I was a woman."

Pili was lucky because her body was brawny and she was an excellent actor. She cursed and talked shit just like the men. She was bold and worked tirelessly. She told an interviewer for UN Women how she drank Konyagi (a local spirit) and joked with the men about which village women she fancied, effortlessly keeping up her disguise. The miners admired "Uncle Hussein" and his natural leadership abilities; they even sought his advice. In fact, she was able to convince some of the men to stop harassing the village women. Pili doing her part to stamp out catcalling while impersonating a foul-mouthed but good-natured prospector warms the heart. Uncle Hussein the ally!

It's impossible not to ponder how much of this was NOT an act. It *was* a performance of sorts when Pili dressed up and pretended to be a man, yes. Her natural leadership skills, her bravery, her tenacity, and her ability to get the job done are not, however, *male* traits, they are simply *Pili*'s traits. But she had to don the male garb to make that palatable and acceptable.

In 1989, after about a year of mining in the guise of a man, Pili's hard work paid off: She hit pay dirt, unearthing two massive clusters of tanzanite. With her windfall, Pili built homes for her family, bought herself new tools, and began to employ others to work for *her*. We love to see it!

Remarkably, it was ten years before Pili's identity was not so much discovered as revealed by Pili herself out of necessity. A local woman reported that she had been raped by some of the miners; Pili was arrested as one of the suspects. In the BBC interview, Pili recalls that when the police showed up at the mine where she worked, "the men who did the rape said: 'This is the man who did it,' and I was taken to the police station." She had no choice but to ask for a woman official to examine her so she could reveal her female identity and prove she was not one of the men who had committed the assault. She was released.

Even when the police revealed her secret, all the men she employed and worked alongside, year after year, couldn't believe she was a woman. They struggled to comprehend a woman behaving so bravely in the mines, one

who had such a filthy mouth, and who, as she hilariously puts it, "acted like a gorilla," always ready for a fight. It was only in 2001, when Pili got married and started a family, that they finally accepted that she was a woman.

Today, in her sixties, Pili has not only built her own lucrative mining company, employing more than 70 workers, but she also has 7 houses, 150 acres of land, 100 cows, and a tractor. Her profits have enabled her to pay for the education of more than 30 nieces, nephews, and grandchildren! Pili's undeniable chutzpah led to her tremendous success, and her achievements in mining went on to inspire dozens of women in Tanzania to reach out in hopes of learning how to start mining businesses of their own. Mining remains an almost exclusively male industry in Tanzania, but because of Pili's literal muscle, she and these women went to the government and asked for support in designating a specific plot where women could mine. No word yet if they have been successful, but I doubt Pili will ever give up trying. Just call her Tenacious P!

BABY YOU WERE BORN TO RUN: THE STORY OF KATHRINE SWITZER

In 1967, twenty-year-old Kathrine Switzer became the first woman to officially enter and run the Boston Marathon. When she registered as K. V. Switzer by mail, she was admitted and given bib numbers, whereas other women, using their full names, tried and were rejected. Switzer didn't use clothing as her way into a place she wasn't supposed to go; rather, the omission of a few letters in her name provided her a ticket to ride . . . er . . . run.

In 1959, young Kathrine wanted to join the cheerleading squad. Her parents had put her in an accelerated school program, so when she headed to high school, she was just edging toward puberty while her classmates were already fully entrenched in the boobs, the pimples, the horniness of it all. In her eyes, being a cheerleader would help her fit in and give her popular points. Her dad protested, "You know, honey, you shouldn't be on

the sidelines cheering for other people. People should cheer for you." He encouraged her to join the girls' field hockey team instead and told her that if she ran a mile every day, she'd be ready by the time tryouts came. She took his advice, and she made the team. In the process, much to her surprise, she fell in love with running.

A bit of history. Women were excluded from participating in the first modern Olympics, in 1896. A big improvement over DEATH, which was the punishment for any woman who even tried to *watch* the ancient Olympic Games. The ancient Greek geographer Pausanias tells the story of the widow Callipateira, who snuck into the games disguised as a man to watch her son compete. When the authorities found out, they didn't execute her, but from that point on, all attendees had to strip, revealing their manhood, before they were permitted into the arena. Really. There's so much to roll one's eyes at here. "Show us your pecker and feel free to enter!"

Eventually, after much protest, women were permitted to compete in the modern Olympics beginning in 1900—in golf, tennis, and croquet only. In 1928, women's track and field was added. That year, the lengthiest event for women was the 800-meter race. After the first female competitors ran a tight race and Lina Radke set a new world record, they all collapsed, spent, on the infield. In her book *Marathon Woman*, Switzer tells us, "This 'display of exhaustion' horrified spectators, officials, and, worse, the media." Harold Abrahams, an Olympic runner turned journalist, scoffed that "this spectacle of exhaustion was a disgrace to womanhood and a danger to all females." He lobbied for the women's 800-meter to be banished from future Olympics. And it was. For thirty-two years.

Cut to the 1960 Olympics in Rome. The 1960 games made a huge impact on thirteen-year-old Switzer because it was the first time since 1928 that the women's 800-meter race was held. Watching the newly reinstated race on TV, Switzer thought, Wow, thirty-two years was how long it took women to convince the powers that be that running a bloody half mile wouldn't ruin them and all humanity. The men could run ALL the races, ALL the distances, and no one was worried about what it would do to *their* bodies or the nuclear family or civilization itself. The longest race of all, of course, was the marathon. It had been a battle just to get the 800 back for women; imagine how the almighty daddies of the world would feel about women running a *marathon*.

By the time Switzer was a nineteen-year-old journalism student at Syracuse University, her running distances were getting longer and longer and she was completely devoted. Back then, running was not the obsessive

---

A marathon is officially 26.2 miles, or 42.2 kilometers. The marathon was one of the original modern Olympic events in 1896 . . . you know, the one I mentioned above—the you-can't-play-here one, NOT the we'll-kill-you-if-you-even-try-to-watch one. And not to get too far ahead of ourselves, but the women's marathon was not introduced at the Olympic Games until (drumroll please) . . . the 1984 Summer Olympics in Los Angeles. NINETEEN. EIGHTY. FOUR. Eighty-eight years after the first modern Olympics. Well, thank God they prevented all those years of lady moustaches, I guess.

The Boston Marathon began in April 1897. It is the world's oldest annual marathon and ranks as one of the most prestigious. The event attracts five hundred thousand spectators each year, making it New England's most widely attended sporting event. It started with fifteen participants in 1897 and now attracts an average of thirty thousand registered participants, about half of whom are women.

---

pastime it is today, but it certainly was not considered a woman's domain. The well-worn myths were that running would cause a woman's legs to get too big, that they'd grow a moustache, and that their reproductive functions would be affected, but that didn't stop Switz, as her close friends were now calling her. She somehow knew all of that was hogwash: "This is really such B.S. . . . If you have children it's going to be much more injurious to your system than running."

There was no women's running team at Switzer's university, or anywhere else for that matter, so she began training with the men's cross-country team and that is where she met Arnie Briggs, a fifty-year-old university mailman and dedicated long-distance runner, who took Switz under his wing to train her.

One night after listening to Arnie wax poetic about the famed Boston Marathon for the umpteenth time—a race he'd run some fifteen times—Switzer finally snapped, "Let's quit *talking* about the Boston Marathon and run the damn thing!" Arnie snapped back that a woman couldn't run that kind of distance. Switzer, however, knew better. She had heard about a woman who *had* run, unofficially, in 1966, the year before: Roberta "Bobbi" Gibb.

There might not be a Kathrine Switzer if there wasn't a Bobbi Gibb. You know that old saying, "So-and-so walked so that so-and-so could run"? Well, Bobbi ran so that Kathrine could run. Gibb (born November 2, 1942) was the first woman to run the entire Boston Marathon. She ran unofficially, unregistered, and without a number pinned to her chest.

A dedicated and exceptional long-distance runner, twenty-four-year-old Bobbi Gibb excitedly mailed off her registration for the Boston Marathon in 1966. Keep in mind, there were no women's running shoes back then, so Bobbi trained in white leather Red Cross nurses' shoes and

I love women so much. Her registration was returned with a note stating not only that she was ineligible to run because she was a woman but also that women were *physiologically incapable* of running the distance. That was when she knew she HAD to run the marathon . . . with or without a number. Eighteen hours after arriving in Massachusetts by bus, Bobbi could be found crouching behind a bush near the starting line. When the runners took off, she waited a moment and then jumped in and joined the pack. Gibb finished in three hours, twenty-one minutes, and forty seconds, besting two-thirds of the other (all male) runners! So much for "physiologically incapable," huh, boys?

Before registering for the 1967 Boston Marathon, Switzer not only had to prove to Arnie that she could run twenty-six miles, but the two of them also made a point of checking what the official rule book said about women. There was zero mention of sex or gender, so they decided they were good to go: Kathrine registered as K. V. Switzer. Race officials would later say that Switzer's registration was a result of an "oversight" in the entry screening process and that she was in "flagrant violation of the rules," making it entirely acceptable that she was treated as an interloper once the error was discovered.

As Switzer began to train more intentionally for Boston, she saw fit to inform her family doctor about her running. According to Switzer, he sat across from her smoking a cigarette and asked, "Why would an attractive woman like you want to run a marathon?" Then he advised her to stop running because it could affect her ability to have kids and—essentially— warned her that her uterus could fall out. And I'm not even joking.

On race day, Switzer stood at the starting line with her fellow racers wearing the number 261 pinned to her chest, a number that would go on to inspire women around the world. She was all set to run with Arnie, a fellow named John from her cross-country team, and Tom, her burly hammer-throwing boyfriend, who had never trained to run long distance in his life, but when Switzer signed up for the marathon he immediately signed up as well, insisting, "If any *girl* can run twenty-six miles, I can do it, too." On race day he insisted Switzer remove her lipstick, mortified that she showed up wearing makeup. Switz refused to remove her lipstick because FUCK OFF, TOM.

In her bestselling book, Switzer describes the scene before the race as jovial. Most of her fellow runners were happy to see a girl there. Then they were off. Everything was going swimmingly, and then around mile four the press truck came along and slowed next to Switzer and her running mates. They were snapping pictures and couldn't get enough of a GIRL running the Boston Marathon.

Suddenly, things took a turn. Switzer describes hearing the unmistakable sound of leather shoes slapping on the pavement behind her, "Instinctively I jerked my head around quickly and looked square into the most vicious face I'd ever seen. A big man, a huge man, with bared teeth was set to pounce, and before I could react he grabbed my shoulder and flung me back, screaming, 'Get the hell out of my race and give me those numbers!' Then he swiped down my front, trying to rip off my bib number, just as I leapt backward from him."

The man was Jock Semple, a sixty-four-year-old Scottish American with anger-management issues and a thick accent, who also happened to be the race director. The photographs of an enraged Semple repeatedly assaulting Switzer as she tried to run are famous and historic, having been published all over the world. The images were burned into my memory from the moment I laid eyes on them.

Arnie yelled at Semple to leave Switzer alone, but he wouldn't stop. That is when Sort of Sexist but Not All Bad Tom the Boyfriend could no longer stand by while someone physically attacked his girlfriend, and he body slammed Semple off Switzer, sending him soaring through the air. Jock meet jock. They all took off running.

bib would have a number on it, but instead of her name it would say UNOFFICIAL. "Then I would finish the race and I would get the unofficial first woman prize and they would award me an unofficial trophy." It sounds ridiculous because it was. AN UNOFFICIAL WOMAN.

As for Semple, while he would eventually support and endorse women running the Boston Marathon, his enlightenment didn't come easy. During a 1970 broadcast from the New York City Marathon, Semple whined, "There's enough competition for women, why do they want to tackle the toughest thing in the world? It's just women and their stubbornness, just want to do something that they're not supposed to do, that's all there is to it!"

A 1968 *Sports Illustrated* feature on Semple written by a male journalist and brimming with sexist commentary includes a quote from Red Auerbach, then general manager of the Celtics: "Now a lot of people laughed at that situation where Jock went after that girl last year, but I didn't. The Boston Marathon is a big part of that man's life. He didn't want a mockery made of something he believes so strongly in." A *mockery*. The article doesn't shy away from detailing Semple's frequent bouts of rage and his inability to control his anger. It chuckles even—oh, what a fiery Scot! The writer goes on to excuse and embrace his temper, reframing it as passion, something to be admired. Jock just cares so damn much about *his* marathon, it's MORE than just a race to him. What Jock Semple and the article can't seem to grasp is the importance and significance of the marathon to these women. Semple's actions were forgiven because of his passion, but no such pass or understanding was given to a woman breaking the rules because of something *she* was passionate about, something *she* believed in, something that was much more than just a race to her.

Things would eventually change for the better, but the backlash immediately following Switzer's Boston run felt punitive and paternalistic. Remember those rule books that made no mention of gender? After Switzer ran with a number, they were quickly changed to specify NO WOMEN. So that's fun. And, yes, Switzer was banned and spent years running as an invited unofficial participant in amateur competitions, proving she was not considered a disgraced leper. But those photos of Semple attacking Switzer went around the world, and the issue of women being barred or limited in how or where they were permitted to run started to get nationwide attention. And it wasn't long before protest and public pressure (and heads being removed from asses) resulted in women finally being allowed to run farther than 800 meters, farther than a mile and a half, farther than ten miles (an interim rule stated that women could run up to ten miles, but they needed special permission to run a marathon). Man, they LOVE to make us ask for permission, don't they? It was not until 1972 that the AAU finally changed its rules and began to sanction women's division marathons.

Switzer's historic run changed everything for her. The manhandling, the photographs, the disqualification, and the ban all solidified her course in life, her activism, and her ambitions. In 2019, she told *Runner's World*, "In the race, I kept wondering why other women didn't run and then it dawned on me that they were afraid to try because they'd been told all these myths of limitation and believed them. I knew if they were offered an opportunity to try, they would respond. And that is what I decided to do with my life, to try to create opportunities and spread the word."

In 2017, seventy-year-old Switzer ran the Boston Marathon, marking the fiftieth anniversary of her historic marathon debut in 1967. Bobbi Gibb served as grand marshal of the event, fifty-one years after becoming the first woman to complete the race. Gibb and Switzer were both honored that year as pioneers in the sport.

DR. MARY EDWARDS WALKER

In the history of the United States, only one woman has received the Medal of Honor: Dr. Mary Edwards Walker. Staunch abolitionist, dress reformer, and eccentric, Walker was the second American woman to graduate from medical school and the first female United States Army surgeon during the Civil War. She was also arrested innumerable times throughout her life for dressing as a man.

Mary Walker was born on November 26, 1832, in Oswego, New York. Her parents were abolitionist "freethinkers" who opened the first free school in Oswego, determined that their daughters be as educated as their son. In addition to her parents demonstrating and encouraging nontraditional gender roles in their home, they were also the first to introduce

Walker to the idea of a more hygienic and health-promoting way for females to dress—namely NOT the usual long skirts, corsets, and tight lacings that were the standard uniform for women of that era.

By the time Walker entered Syracuse Medical College in 1853, she would have been sporting some version of the progressive "bloomers" outfit that consisted of loose trousers with a midlength dress overtop. She was criticized by men and women alike and was even chased down the street once by a pack of boys who threw eggs at her. For wearing pants. Unflappable, Walker went on to graduate with honors in 1855. She was the only woman in her graduating class and only the second woman to receive a medical degree in America, after Dr. Elizabeth Blackwell.

When the Civil War broke out in 1861, twenty-nine-year-old Walker was determined to be of service. She went to Washington to enlist as a surgeon, much to the shock of the men in charge, who not only rejected her but made a big stink about it, too. Secretary of War Simon Cameron found Walker's request *and* her trousers-under-a-dress to be absurd and dismissed her. Undeterred, Mary was like, FINE, you won't give me an *official* placement? I'll just sign up as an unpaid volunteer surgeon— TRY AND STOP ME FROM HELPING. Once again, we see women participating and contributing . . . but in an *unofficial* capacity.

Walker could have posed as a man, like the nearly four hundred women who enlisted and fought during the Civil War, but that was never an option for her. Eschewing the expected feminine traits of the day, namely shyness and humility, Mary *wanted* recognition as a female, and concealing her sex would have negated that goal. Again and again in her story, we see that Mary wanted and demanded to be seen and accepted, to have her achievements acknowledged. We cannot underestimate how terrifically bold that was for a woman of that time and how many young women she may have influenced simply through her visibility. Representation matters!

In 1862, Walker transferred to an outpost in Virginia and was treating wounded soldiers near the front lines. She continued to ask for an official commission as a surgeon and was gaining notoriety. The *New York Tribune* singled out her achievements, going so far as to dunk on the military's reluctance to legitimize her, asking, "What 'ism' is more absurd than Conservatism? If a woman is proved competent for duty, and anxious to perform it, why restrain her?" *Swoosh.*

One can't help but imagine how much innovation and excellence were flat-out denied throughout history because white men were like, no thank you, we don't want that from *you*. We have our collective fingers in our ears, and we don't wish to hear about your female (or Black, or queer) excellence.

In 1863, Walker's request—er, relentless demands accompanied by some public shaming in the press—was finally approved. She became the first female United States Army surgeon, a "Contract Acting Assistant Surgeon (civilian)," in Ohio. Finally, Walker wore the sanctioned dress of a Union military surgeon, sporting the same uniform as her male counterparts. Proud of her achievement, Walker wrote, "I let my curls grow while I was in the army so that everybody would know that I was a woman." Come on, curls!

Walker had a big mouth, and she rubbed many men the wrong way— they had likely never encountered a woman like her before, but her reputation for being a top-tier surgeon also got around. She spoke out about how frequently frontline surgeons were performing unnecessary amputations. She counseled wounded soldiers about their right to refuse such surgeries and stepped in to help save many a limb. Her belief that amputation should be the absolute last option made her beloved by the troops.

In April 1864, Walker had just finished assisting a surgery when she was captured by Confederate soldiers. She was held as a prisoner of war for four months at Castle Thunder, a filthy and overcrowded Confederate prison in Richmond, Virginia. One Confederate captain wrote to his wife that they were "both amused and disgusted at the sight of a thing that nothing but the debased and depraved Yankee nation could produce . . . she was dressed in the full uniform of a Federal Surgeon . . . not good looking and of course had tongue enough for a regiment of men." RECORD SCRATCH. *Tongue enough for a regiment of men?* Yes, please! Don't you wish you could've heard how she dished it out to these guys?

At the end of the war, this boss lady lobbied for a brevet promotion to major. I love that she asked for what she felt she deserved! It would have been so momentous for a woman to stand up and say, "Give me this, I earned it." Secretary of War Edwin Stanton did not grant the request, but President Andrew Johnson, well aware of Walker's achievements, was determined to find another way to recognize her service. He presented Walker with the Medal of Honor for Meritorious Service in 1865, expressing that she "devoted herself with patriotic zeal to the sick and wounded soldiers, both in the field and hospital, to the detriment of her own health, and has also endured hardships as a prisoner-of-war four months in a Southern prison." Wonderful! Only wait . . .

In 1917, Congress decided to up and change the eligibility requirements for the Medal of Honor—an attempt to reduce the long list of pension recipients—to include only those who had engaged in "actual combat with an enemy." So, saving many lives and countless limbs and being a prisoner of war for four months counts as nothing? Oh, okay, *cool.* Mary's medal was rescinded, and they asked for it back. I'm sorry, that is shocking. They asked for it back? Friends, did Dr. Mary Edwards Walker do as asked?

SHE CERTAINLY DID NOT. She wore it proudly and intentionally on her lapel every day until her death.

After the war, Mary had more time than ever to devote to her biggest passion: dress reform. She believed that the fight for women's rights hinged on the very clothes on their backs. In their obituary, the *New York Times* lauded her dedication to "advocating with her strange eloquence the emancipation of the sex and the assumption of men's attire as the first practical step."

Freedom to Walker meant, first and foremost, freedom of movement, which we hear about again and again in this book and which my elasticized-waist-loving self completely understands! In her 1871 book, *Hit*, Walker elucidates everything problematic with women's dress of her era: It's terrible for circulation; the dresses are too long, running along the ground spreading germs and disease; the corsets squish internal organs, causing pain and injury; the popular hairstyles are too tight and akin to torture. How, she asks, can a woman formulate intelligent thoughts in her head when she is so preoccupied with the hairs atop it? In response to the oft-admired "womanly sway" that resulted when a corseted and hoop-skirted lady walked by, she scoffed, "It would soon be manly enough, if men carried the burdens of dress in the same way that women do." (As a devoted viewer of *RuPaul's Drag Race*, I can attest to this assertion!)

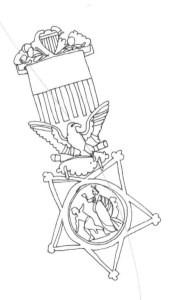

Dr. Walker insisted that obtaining the right to vote was nothing when compared to what standard feminine dress was doing to keep a woman down: "The greatest sorrows from which women suffer today are those physical, moral, and mental ones, that are caused by their unhygienic manner of dressing! The want of the *ballot* is but a *toy* in comparison!"

In the latter part of her life, Dr. Walker only wore trousers, suits, and her customary top hat, not even *trying* to play nice and wear a sort-of dress anymore. Like everything in her life, it was a political statement. "I don't wear men's clothes, I wear my own clothes," she told the *Vineland Independent* in 1880. She was frequently arrested for impersonating a man and would shame the men in the courtroom, telling them she should be able to wear whatever she wanted after putting her life on the line during the war. YES, MA'AM! The final time she was arrested, the judge famously dismissed the case and ordered the police never to arrest Dr. Walker on that charge again. She left the courtroom to enthusiastic applause.

"Dr. Mary Walker, Crusader, Is Dead" read the *New York Times* headline on February 23, 1919. When she died at the age of eighty-seven, Mary, unsurprisingly, was buried in a black suit so she could be as comfortable in death as she was in life.

Nearly sixty years after her death, at the urging of Walker's great-grandniece, the Army Board for Correction of Military Records reviewed the circumstances surrounding the revocation of Dr. Walker's Medal of Honor. On June 19, 1977, the board approved the recommendation to restore Dr. Walker's medal, acknowledging her "distinguished gallantry, self-sacrifice, patriotism, dedication, and unflinching loyalty to her country, despite the apparent discrimination because of her sex." She remains the sole female recipient of the Medal of Honor.

PIRATES
ANNE BONNY AND
MARY READ

While there are many conflicting reports surrounding the lives of Anne Bonny and Mary Read, the veracity of their existence should not be up for debate. As Captain Charles Johnson wrote in his *A General History of the Pyrates* (1724), "The Truth of it can be no more contested, than that there were such Men in the World, as Roberts and Black-beard, who were Pyrates."

Anne Bonny was born in County Cork, Ireland, about 1700. She was conceived when her lawyer father, William Cormac, got busy with the family maid, Mary Brennan. Her father grew so fond of Anne that he took her in, but to avoid scandal, he dressed her as a boy and said she was a

relative's son. He called her "Andy" and lied to his wife, saying he was mentoring the boy to be a lawyer's clerk. Mr. and Mrs. Cormac's marriage was already on thin ice when this went down, but William was motivated to keep the marriage afloat since he was getting a sizable allowance from his wife's fortune. However, when Mrs. Cormac discovered the truth about who young Andy was, the marriage was once and for all kaput, as was William's endowment.

William Cormac, free of his loveless-but-profitable marriage, grabbed Anne, no longer dressed as a boy, and Mary, his former servant/baby mama, and set sail for North America, settling in Charleston (Charles Town) about 1708. The Irish are inextricably linked to the establishment of Charleston as Irish immigrants began landing in South Carolina as early as 1669. By the time our trio arrived, Charleston was still a relatively new settlement, having been established in 1670, but it was bustling with growth. To give you an idea of why and how the town was so "bustling," the population of Charleston in 1708 was 9,580 and more than 4,000 of those humans were enslaved. South Carolina was a "slave society," with slavery being central to its economy.

Anne's life was changed forever when her mother died, likely from typhoid fever, when Anne was about fourteen or fifteen years old. The Carolinians may have excelled at oppressing fellow humans for economic growth, but oppressing bacteria and disease proved a bit more challenging. Did you know doctors didn't even start washing their hands until the mid-nineteenth century? (Shudder.) Burdened by the considerable responsibility of being the woman of the house, Anne soon began to act out and was known to have a "hot Irish temper." She began consorting with drunks and sailors. Her father eventually had enough when he discovered that Anne had married penniless seaman James Bonny. Cormac disowned Anne and threw her out of the house.

Sometime between 1715 and 1718, Anne and James sailed to Nassau on the Isle of New Providence (now the Bahamas). Nassau, a known sanctuary for marauders of the seas, was deemed the Republic of Pirates between 1706 and 1718. I'm guessing moving to a place known as the Republic of Pirates was no accident, but it doesn't sound as if our happy couple was on the same page, goal-wise. Anne showed no signs of stopping her carousing once in Nassau, while James began to rise in the ranks as an informant, reporting on—you guessed it—pirates. Anne was so steeped in antiestablishment contrarianism at this point that she took her fraternizing to the next level and, much to her husband's dismay, started mingling with pirates. One of those pirates met his match in fiery Anne Bonny: the infamous Calico Jack himself, Captain John Rackham. Before long it was "seems like old times" for Anne when Jack had her dress up as a man so she could run off with him and join his pirate crew.

Incredibly, Anne Bonny and Mary Read ended up on the same pirate ship, disguised as men. Also incredibly, they were both illegitimate daughters who were dressed as boys by parents looking out for their own self-interests. I mean, that is WILD. What are the odds that the two would be dressed as little boys by their parents and then also end up as cross-dressing pirates on the same ship? ("Of all the pirate ships in all the oceans in all the world, she walks onto mine.")

Mary Read was also a bastardy child. That is a legal term, I'm not being mean! Born in 1685 in England, her mother passed her off as a son who had died in order to keep receiving financial support from the family of her deceased son's father. Even when that ruse was up, Mary continued dressing as a boy because it was the only way to get odd jobs and make some extra cash. Her mother got her a job as a "footboy" to help support the family. Footboys were servants who ran alongside the carriages of wealthy women to make sure the ride went smoothly. First, what a job! Second, imagine Mary's quads!

Recognizing the upward mobility that dude-ness offered her, Mary kept up her disguise and eventually joined the Royal Navy. She soon tired of the navy and moved to Flanders and joined the army there. In Flanders, she fell in love with a Flemish soldier she was stationed with. Of course, the history books love to sprinkle in some light homophobia about how *relieved* the Flemish soldier was when he found out that he wasn't attracted to another man, that Mary was actually a woman. *Oh please.* I bet military men since the dawn of time have been boinking each other and understood sexual fluidity long before any of us were listening to a damn podcast about it.

Mary got out of her breeches and married the Flemish soldier, whose name was never logged into the annals of history. They both left the army, and they opened a tavern together in Breda called The Three Horseshoes. Sadly, the Flemish husband died, and Mary soon lost the tavern. Preferring not to starve, she went back to what she possibly knew best: She started dressing as a man, and when the opportunity arose, she jumped at the chance to board a ship headed for the West Indies, determined to start over (again!) in a new environment. It would have been a very new start, indeed, for that ship was taken over by pirates, and when given the choice of join or die, Mary signed up willingly. Say what you will about Mary Read, the woman knew how to pivot.

Pirating was getting out of control and the authorities were at a loss about how to deal with what was becoming quite the strain on big business. On September 5, 1717, King George I of Great Britain issued the "Proclamation for Suppressing of Pirates," granting full pardon of all crimes to pirates who surrendered to any governor in the colonies within the year. Mary Read is documented as taking the king's pardon, but by 1720 she was a known member of Calico Jack's crew, so obviously Mary wasn't quite done with that thug life.

Reports vary about how and when Mary Read and Anne Bonny met, but the consensus seems to be that it was aboard the *Revenge*, Calico Jack's ship.

Jack and his crew took over a ship Mary was pirating on, and, just like before, instead of being thrown overboard, Mary went the "if you can't beat 'em and you don't want to be murdered by them, join 'em!" route and officially joined Calico Jack's crew. Legend has it that Anne was immediately attracted to "Mark," the young man Mary was posing as. Anne, also still disguised as a man, had designs on seducing the new guy and pulled him aside to reveal her ample bosom only to discover . . . *another* ample bosom and a new BFF! Whether this story is 100 percent factual or it's the eighteenth-century version of let's beef up this story with some girl-on-girl action, we'll never know.

Mary Read was ruthless, a lionhearted fighter with a filthy mouth. None of the crew, including Calico Jack, suspected she was a woman. In fact, Jack was even jealous, observing that his lover, Anne, was hot for "Mark." Before he got jealous enough to accidentally stab the new guy in the dick, Mary thought it wise to reveal her identity to Jack, and, like his lady Anne, he swore to keep her secret.

During battles, Mary and Anne fought side by side, doing their best to have each other's backs. It's not clear if everyone aboard was fooled about them being boys or if it was more of a "don't ask don't tell" situation, especially since the women were favored by the fearsome captain himself. Victims who were witnesses at their trials declared "that both women 'were very active on Board, and willing to do any Thing'" and that they were "very profligate, cursing and swearing much, and very ready and willing." If their fellow crew members *did* know the truth about them, they likely didn't care because these bitches got shit done.

In late 1720, as the Golden Age of Piracy was about to come to an end and as their ship was about to be overtaken, it was only Anne and Mary who refused to give up and kept fighting to the end. Both were disgusted by their fellow crew members, who cowered or surrendered. The epic tale has the fierce ladies remaining on deck and facing the invaders alone, firing their pistols and swinging their cutlasses. Mary, appalled by her cowardly crewmates, peered over the entrance of the hold and yelled, "If there's a man among ye, ye'll come up and fight like the man ye are to be!" When no one responded, she fired into the hold, killing one and wounding others. When tenacious Anne and Mary could no longer hold off their assailants, everyone was taken prisoner.

The lot of them were brought to trial in what is now Spanish Town, Jamaica, where they were sentenced to hang for acts of piracy. Anne's famous last words to Calico Jack were, "If you had fought like a man, you need not have been hang'd like a dog." *Damn.* Mary and Anne were also sentenced to hang, but as they were no longer disguised as men, they took full advantage of the situation and both claimed to be with child (known as "pleading the belly," which is a term I shall now use when anyone inquires why I favor elasticized waists). Both received stays of execution, and reportedly they *were* both found to be pregnant. Mary developed a fever and died in prison. As for Anne Bonny's fate, there is no shortage of speculation. Some suggest that Bonny gave birth while in custody, while others say she returned to Charleston, where she had eight children. The *Oxford Dictionary of National Biography* reports that her wealthy father secured her release with a bribe, taking her back to South Carolina, where she died in April 1782. What we do know is that there is no record of Bonny's release or execution. *A General History of the Pyrates* wraps up Anne's story: "She was continued in Prison, to the Time of her lying in, and afterwards reprieved from Time to Time; but what is become of her since, we cannot tell; only this we know, that she was not executed." Talk about Lady Luck.

ACKNOWLEDGMENTS

Let me begin by saying how grateful I am for my agent, Rhea Lyons, who is so much more than a literary agent. She is a cheerleader, a hand-holder, a safe person to have a cry with, an enthusiastic audience, and a next-level proofreader. This book would not be without her. Thank you also to Julia Kardon, who effortlessly stepped in as cheerleader and agent extraordinaire when Rhea had to step away to have the cutest baby on the Eastern Seaboard. And to my editor, Liz Sullivan, who immediately had a vision for what this book could be and came after it with gusto, which I will always be grateful for.

I must thank my stellar group of friends. My chosen family. My loves. I am beyond lucky to have such smart and generous people in my life, many of whom read chapters in their nascent stage and gave brilliant feedback. Thank you for (almost) always taking my calls and talking me through more than a couple of meltdowns: Thom Payne, Kelli Fox, J. Paul Halferty, Laura Eichhorn, Amy Sloan, Jeanie Calleja, Mary Pat Farrell, Scott Smith, and Neil Katcher.

Thank you to sweet pal, author, and TV writer Hollie Overton for walking me through so many unknowns and taking my calls when I was but a stranger with a million questions.

Thank you to my birthday and spiritual twin Kathleen Munroe, who just means so much to me. Thank you for always being my number one reader and my biggest champion.

I was deeply fortunate to connect with author, professor, activist, and all-around wonderful human Melody Moezzi, who offered her time and energy so generously and lovingly.

Thank you so much to Alex Schmider of GLAAD, who generously consulted with me and gave such wise and insightful feedback.

I want to thank filmmaker Kate Novack, whose short film *Hysterical Girl* was so well done and so inspiring. And thank you to social media for allowing me to connect with lovely Kate, which led to us talking all things "hysteria." Please find and watch her film.

Many heartfelt thanks to writer Emma Garman, who graciously and generously shared her sources for Margaret King with me and whose excellent profile of King should be sought out and devoured (it's on Longreads!).

Thank you to Trina Robbins, Catherine Nichols, Gail Simone, Liz Denlinger of the NYPL, Allana Harkin, Hannah Popal, and of course to Carrie Hannigan for forwarding my email to Rhea back in 2019.

Thank you to the province of Nova Scotia for safeguarding my sanity for a time during the writing process. If I could marry a province, I would marry you.

I'm still pinching myself that I was able to get the phenomenal Tina Berning to make art for this book. Tina, I am in love with you as an artist and a human. I hope we get to do this again.

Thank you to Fran Lebowitz, who allowed young me to marvel at smart snark and to see and hear myself in her writing and who helped me understand the importance of a navy blazer.

Thank you to my brother, Greg Dawson, and my mom and dad, Lise Dawson and the late Robert Dawson, for all their love and support through the years. You know, it can't be easy having a child who wants to first work in the theater, then in comedy, then in television . . . watching the child face immeasurable rejection and living a feast-or-famine lifestyle. But my parents accepted my career choices (after it became clear there was no talking me out of them) and became my biggest fans. They sat through several awkward comedy shows and helped me pay rent a couple of times in my early days and did things like drive halfway across Canada to see me in a musical. When I started booking regular jobs and winning awards, their glowing pride and relief were so gratifying.

My mom is a tenacious woman who taught me how to ask for a better hotel room when they try to stick you in something subpar. She held lots of different jobs in her life and showed me it's okay to be good at different things and to reinvent yourself and to stay curious. I wish my dad were here to see this, he would be so proud, telling the fellas down at the pub about me and the book.

I am really proud of myself that I wrote this book. And that I did so during arguably one of the hardest moments in recent history. This book began as an idea for a television project and then one day I thought it could be a book and now it *is* a book! I'm proud of myself! And I'm proud of you. You read all the way to the end of the acknowledgments, good job!

I remain eternally grateful to women. The greatest lie the devil ever told (and that was made into gospel) is that *we* are the weak ones. What a joke.

SELECTED BIBLIOGRAPHY

Abbott, Karen. "If There's a Man Among Ye: The Tale of Pirate Queens Anne Bonny and Mary Read." *Smithsonian Magazine*. August 9, 2011. https://www.smithsonianmag.com/history/if-theres-a-man-among-ye-the-tale-of-pirate-queens-anne-bonny-and-mary-read-45576461/ (accessed June 23, 2021).

Abott, Lynn, and Doug Seroff. *Out of Sight: The Rise of African American Popular Music, 1899–1895*. Jackson: University Press of Mississippi, 2009.

Alaei, Forough. "Undercover: Female Football Fans in Iran." *The Guardian*. April 15, 2019. https://www.theguardian.com/artanddesign/2019/apr/15/undercover-female-football-fans-in-iran (accessed June 15, 2021).

Allen-Smith, Natascha. "Cross-Dressing, Elopement and Travels with Percy Shelley: The Extraordinary Life of Margaret King." Leeds Museums & Galleries. October 24, 2018. https://museumsandgalleries.leeds.gov.uk/collections/cross-dressing-elopement-and-travels-with-percy-shelley-the-extraordinary-life-of-margaret-king/ (accessed August 18, 2020).

An-Nai'm, Abdullahi Ahmed. "Sharia Law." Muslims for Progressive Values. https://www.mpvusa.org/sharia-law (accessed July 6, 2021).

Appleby, John C. *Women and English Piracy, 1540–1720: Partners and Victims of Crime*. Woodbridge, Suffolk, UK: Boydell Press, 2015.

Aresti, Nerea. "The Gendered Identities of the 'Lieutenant Nun': Rethinking the Story of a Female Warrior in Early Modern Spain." *Gender & History* (John Wiley & Sons) 19, no. 3 (November 2007): 401–418.

Aronson, James. "Meet the Real Miss Fury—It's All Done with Mirrors." *New York Post*. April 6, 1942. Quoted in Allan Holtz, "Ink-Slinger Profiles: Tarpé Mills." http://strippersguide.blogspot.com/2012/06/ink-slinger-profiles-tarpe-mills.html?m=0 (accessed June 15, 2021).

"Baillie, Joanna (1762–1851)." Encyclopedia.com. March 24, 2020. https://www.encyclopedia.com/arts/culture-magazines/baillie-joanna-1762-1851 (accessed March 24, 2020).

Balkun, Mary McAleer, and Susan C. Imbarrato, eds. *Women's Narratives of the Early Americas and the Formation of Empire*. New York: Palgrave, 2016.

Barber, Nicholas. "Remembering Miss Fury—The World's First Great Superheroine." BBC. March 29, 2021. https://www.bbc.com/culture/article/20210329-remembering-miss-fury-the-worlds-first-great-superheroine (accessed June 15, 2021).

Barrett, W. P. *The Trial of Jeanne d'Arc*. Translated by Coley Taylor and Ruth H. Kerr. New York: Gotham House, 1932. Accessed at "Medieval Sourcebook: The Trial of Joan of Arc," Fordham University. https://sourcebooks.fordham.edu/basis/joanofarc-trial.asp (accessed February 21, 2021).

Baudelaire, Charles. *Mon coeur mis à nu*. Createspace, 2014. Quoted selection translated by Tracy Dawson, 2021.

Blanton, Deanne. "Cathay Williams: Black Woman Soldier, 1866–68." In *Buffalo Soldiers in the West: A Black Soldiers Anthology*, edited by Bruce A. Glasrud and Michael N. Searles, 101–13. College Station: Texas A&M University Press, 2007.

Borden, Carol. "Miss Fury and Miss Mills." Cultural Gutter. March 24, 2016. https://culturalgutter.com/2016/03/24/miss-fury-and-miss-mills/ (accessed June 23, 2021).

Broderick, Marian. *Wild Irish Women: Extraordinary Lives from History*. Dublin: O'Brien Press, 2001.

Brontë, Charlotte. *The Letters of Charlotte Brontë: 1848–1851*. Edited by Margaret Smith. Vol. 2. Oxford: University of Oxford Press, 2000.

Brooks, Libby. "Calls for Memorial to Scotland's Tortured and Executed Witches." *The Guardian*. October 29, 2019. https://www.theguardian.com/uk-news/2019/oct/29/calls-for-memorial-to-scotlands-tortured-and-executed-witches (accessed February 11, 2020).

Bryant, Myffanwy. "The Extraordinary Circumnavigation of Jeanne Baret." Australian National Maritime Museum. July 27, 2020. https://www.sea.museum/2020/07/27/the-extraordinary-circumnavigation-of-jeanne-baret (accessed October 26, 2020).

Burfoot, Amy. "At the Boston Marathon, Leading the Way for Women Fifty Years Ago." *New York Times*. April 16, 2016. https://www.nytimes.com/2016/04/17/sports/at-the-boston-marathon-leading-the-way-for-womenfifty-years-ago.html (accessed June 15, 2021).

Burroughs, Catherine B. *Closet Stages: Joanna Baillie and the Theater Theory of British Romantic Women Writers*. Philadelphia: University of Pennsylvania Press, 1997.

"Cambridge University Anti-Women Students 'Confetti and Rockets' Digitised." BBC. August 11, 2018. https://www.bbc.com/news/uk-england-cambridgeshire-45096690 (accessed March 26, 2020).

Casey, Kathleen. "Cross-Dressers and Race-Crossers: Intersections of Gender and Race in American Vaudeville, 1900–1930." PhD thesis, University of Rochester, 2010.

"Cathay Williams." National Park Service. January 15, 2020. https://www.nps.gov/people/cwilliams.htm (accessed June 11, 2021).

Christensen, Thomas. "Getting Henry." Right Reading (author's personal site). http://www.rightreading.com/henry.handel.richardson/getting-henry-2.htm (accessed March 7, 2020).

Clode, Daniella. *In Search of the Woman Who Sailed the World*. Sydney: Pan Macmillan Australia, 2020.

Coe, Alexis. "Mary Walker's Quest to be Appointed as a Union Doctor in the Civil War." *The Atlantic*. February 7, 2013. https://www.theatlantic.com/sexes/archive/2013/02/mary-walkers-quest-to-be-appointed-as-a-union-doctor-in-the-civil-war/272909/ (accessed June 15, 2021).

Colby, Vineta. *Vernon Lee: A Literary Biography*. Charlottesville: University of Virginia Press, 2003.

Cooney, Kara. *The Woman Who Would Be King: Hatshepsut's Rise to Power in Ancient Egypt*. New York: Crown, 2014.

Cope, Myron. "Angry Overseer of the Marathon Jock Semple, the Colorful Scot Who Manages Boston's Epic Event, Wages a Passionate Battle for His Race and Against Those Who Mock It." *Sports Illustrated*. April 22, 1968. https://vault.si.com/vault/1968/04/22/angry-overseer-of-the-marathon (accessed June 15, 2021).

Craft, William, Ellen Craft, and S. S. Schoff. *Running A Thousand Miles for Freedom: Or, the Escape of William and Ellen Craft from Slavery*. London: William Tweedie, 1860. https://www.google.com/books/edition/Running_a_Thousand_Miles_for_Freedom/C50TAAAAYAAJ?hl=en&gbpv=0 (accessed August 10, 2020).

Davis, Stanford L. "Female Buffalo Soldier—With Documents." Excerpt from Buffalo Soldiers & Indian Wars. 2002. https://www.buffalosoldier.netCathayWilliamsFemaleBuffaloSoldierWithDocuments.htm (accessed June 26, 2020).

de Erauso, Catalina. *Lieutenant Nun: Memoir of a Basque Trans-vestite in the New World*. Translated by Michele Stepto and Gabriel Stepto. Boston: Beacon Press, 1996.

"Disguised Women Sneak into Iranian Football Match." BBC. May 1, 2018. https://www.bbc.com/news/world-middle-east-43964178 (accessed June 8, 2021).

Djossa, Christina Ayele. "The First (Documented) Black Woman to Serve in the U.S. Army." Atlas Obscura. February 28, 2018. https://www.atlasobscura.com/articles/cathay-williams-buffalo-soldier (accessed July 4, 2020).

"Dr. Mary Walker, Crusader, Is Dead; Women's Rights Advocate, Who Wore Male Attire by Authority of Congress, Was 87." *New York Times*. February 23, 1919. https://timesmachine.nytimes.com/timesmachine/1919/02/23/97077779.html?pageNumber=18 (accessed June 15, 2021).

Druitt, Joan. *She Captains: Heroines and Hellions of the Sea*. New York: Simon & Schuster, 2000.

Epstein, Sonia Shechet. "*Hysterical Girl*: Kate Novack on Freud and 'Me Too.'" Science & Film. Museum of the Moving Image. April 21, 2020. http://www.scienceandfilm.org/articles/3304/hysterical-girl-kate-novack -on-freud-and-me-too (accessed December 2020).

Ewan, Elizabeth, Rose Pipes, Jane Rendall, and Siân Reynolds, eds. *The New Biographical Dictionary of Scottish Women*. 2nd ed. Edinburgh: Edinburgh University Press, 2018.

Fein, Esther B. "An Author's Look at 1940's Harlem Is Being Reissued." *New York Times*. January 8, 1992. https://www.nytimes.com/1992/01/08/books/an-author-s-look-at-1940-s-harlem-is-being-reissued.html (accessed June 22, 2021).

Felts, Susannah J. "Alice in Genderland." Chicago Reader. November 2, 2006. https://www.chicagoreader.com/ chicago/alice-in-genderland/Content?oid=923514 (accessed June 19, 2021).

"The Female Soldier: Or, the Surprising Life and Adventures of Hannah Snell." London: R. Walker, 1750. Accessed at Project Gutenberg, June 18, 2011. https://www.gutenberg.org/files/36461/36461-h/36461-h.htm (July 17, 2020).

Garman, Emma. "A Liberated Woman: The Story of Margaret King." Longreads. May 2016. https://longreads .com/2016/05/24/a-liberated-woman-the-story-of-margaret-king/#more-34018 (accessed July 6, 2021).

Gordon, Charlotte. *Romantic Outlaws: The Extraordinary Lives of Mary Wollstonecraft & Mary Shelley*. New York: Random House, 2016.

Gordon, Lyndall. *Charlotte Brontë: A Passionate Life*. New York: W. W. Norton, 1996.

———. *Vindication: A Life of Mary Wollstonecraft*. New York: HarperCollins, 2006.

———. "Yours Insincerely, Charlotte Bronte." *Independent*. July 21, 1995. https://www.independent.co.uk/ arts-entertainment/books/yours-insincerely-charlotte-bronte-1592617.html (accessed April 2, 2020).

Harman, Claire. *Charlotte Brontë: A Fiery Heart*. New York: Alfred A. Knopf, 2016.

Harris, Sharon M. *Dr. Mary Walker: An American Radical*. New Brunswick, NJ: Rutgers University Press, 2009.

Herman, Judith Lewis. *Trauma and Recovery*. New York: Basic Books, 1992.

Holmes, Marian Smith. "The Great Escape from Slavery of Ellen and William Craft." *Smithsonian Magazine*. June 16, 2010. https://www.smithsonianmag.com/history/the-great-escape-from-slavery-of-ellen-and-william -craft-497960/ (accessed October 15, 2019).

Hughes, Kathryn. *George Eliot: The Last Victorian*. New York: Cooper Square Press, 2001.

Hussein, Pili. "From Where I Stand: I Became a Man, Just to Access the Mines." Interview with UN Women. February 23, 2017. https://www.unwomen.org/en/news/stories/2017/2/from-where-i-stand-pili-hussein (accessed June 23, 2021).

———. "I Dressed as a Man to Work in a Mine." Interview with BBC Outlook. April 20, 2017. https://www.bbc.co.uk/programmes/p04ztmnk (accessed June 23, 2021).

Hustvedt, Astri. *Medical Muses: Hysteria in Nineteenth-Century Paris.* New York: W. W. Norton, 2011.

"Infamy and Infidelity." Notes on a Gentleman. July 23, 2019. https://notesonagentleman.substack.com/ (accessed February 5, 2021).

"Iranian Women—Before and After the Islamic Revolution." BBC. February 8, 2019. https://www.bbc.com/news/world-middle-east-47032829 (accessed June 15, 2021).

Ishida, Yoriko. "Hannah Snell: Cross-Dressing Ideology in 18th-Century Naval Culture." THINK.IAFOR. December 12, 2018. https://think.iafor.org/hannah-snell-cross-dressing-ideology-in-18th-century-naval-culture/ (accessed February 10, 2020).

Johnson, Captain Charles. *A General History of the Pyrates, from Their First Rise and Settlement in the Island of Province to the Present Time.* 1724. Project Gutenberg, August 25, 2012. https://www.gutenberg.org/files/40580/40580-h/40580-h.htm (accessed June 15, 2021).

Kapsalis, Terri. "Hysteria, Witches, and the Wandering Uterus: A Brief History." Literary Hub. April 5, 2017. https://lithub.com/hysteria-witches-and-the-wandering-uterus-a-brief-history/ (accessed February 28, 2021).

Kenny, Dylan. "Between Me and My Real Self: On Vernon Lee." *Paris Review.* April 3, 2018. https://www.theparisreview.org/blog/2018/04/03/between-me-and-my-real-self-on-vernon-lee/ (accessed March 26, 2020).

Knight, Alisha R. "Furnace Blasts for the Tuskegee Wizard: Revisiting Pauline Elizabeth Hopkins, Booker T. Washington and the 'Colored American Magazine.'" *American Periodicals* 17, no. 1 (2007): 41–64.

Lawrence, Dorothy. *Sapper Dorothy Lawrence: The Only English Woman Soldier, Late Royal Engineers, 51st Division, 179th Tunnelling Company, B.E.F.* London: John Lane, 1919. https://books.google.com/books?vid=Harvard:32044019016161 (June 23, 2021).

Lewis, Jone Johnson. "About Ellen Craft." ThoughtCo. July 3, 2019. https://www.thoughtco.com/ellen-craft-biography-4068382 (accessed October 15, 2019).

Lindsay, Dunya. "What's in a Name?: Authorship, Autobiography, and Henry Handel Richardson's 'Myself When Young.'" *Antipodes* (Wayne State University Press) 24, no. 1 (June 2010): 49–54.

Maitzen, Rohan. "Second Glance: Her Hands Full of Sugarplums." Open Letters Monthly. https://www
.openlettersmonthlyarchive.com/second-glance/second-glance-her-hands-full-of-sugar-plums
(accessed March 4, 2021).

Marshall, Gail. "Queen Victoria and George Eliot in 1859." *Journal of Victorian Culture* (Leeds Trinity
University) 24, no. 4 (October 2019): 426–30.

McAleer, Edward C. *The Sensitive Plant: A Life of Lady Mount Cashell*. Chapel Hill: University of North
Carolina Press, 1958.

McDermott, Sarah. "I Acted as a Man to Get Work—Until I Was Accused of Rape." BBC. May 15, 2017.
https://www.bbc.com/news/magazine-39705424 (accessed June 14, 2018).

Mead, Rebecca. "George Eliot's Ugly Beauty." *New Yorker*. September 19, 2013. https://www.newyorker.com/
books/page-turner/george-eliots-ugly-beauty (accessed April 15, 2020).

Mendieta, Eva. *In Search of Catalina de Erauso: The National and Sexual Identity of the Lieutenant Nun*.
Translated by Angeles Prado. Reno: Center for Basque Studies, University of Nevada, 2009.

Mesch, Rachel. "Clothes Make the (Wo)man? Pants Permits in Nineteenth-Century Paris." Wonders
& Marvels. http://www.wondersandmarvels.com/2015/09/clothes-make-the-woman-pants-permits-in
-nineteenth-century-paris.html (accessed April 7, 2020).

Miller, Monica L. *Slaves to Fashion: Black Dandyism and the Styling of Black Diasporic Identity*. Durham, NC:
Duke University Press, 2009.

Mills, Tarpé. *Miss Fury: Sensational Sundays 1941–1944*. Edited by Trina Robbins. San Diego, CA: IDW
Publishing, 2013.

Minster, Christopher. "Facts about Anne Bonny and Mary Read, Fearsome Female Pirates." ThoughtCo.
August 19, 2018. https://www.thoughtco.com/facts-about-anne-bonny-mary-read-2136281
(accessed August 1, 2020).

Moore, Margaret King. *A Grandmother's Advice to Young Mothers on the Physical Education of Children*.
Florence: Jos. Molini, 1835. https:/books.google.com/books?id=BKc-jbHK3RQC&source=gbs_navlinks_s
(December 14, 2020).

Mullan, John. *Anonymity: A Secret History of English Literature*. Princeton, NJ: Princeton University Press, 2007.

Murphy, Sam. "Who is Kathrine Switzer and How Did She Change Women's Running?" *Runner's World*.
March 7, 2019. https://www.runnersworld.com/uk/training/motivation/a773110/qa-kathrine-switzer/
(accessed June 15, 2021).

Nagy, Evie. "Heroine Chic: Tarpé Mills' 'Miss Fury.'" *Los Angeles Review of Books*. January 12, 2012. https://lareviewofbooks.org/article/heroine-chic-tarpe-mills-miss-fury/ (accessed September 4, 2020).

Nelson, Camilla. "Hidden Women of History: Tarpé Mills, 1940s Comic Writer, and Her Feisty Superhero Miss Fury." The Conversation. February 4, 2019. https://theconversation.com/hidden-women-of-history -tarpe-mills-1940s-comic-writer-and-her-feisty-superhero-miss-fury-110179 (accessed September 2, 2020).

Neustatter, Angela. "I Know How Elena Ferrante Feels: My Great-Aunt Was Outed Too." *The Guardian*. October 4, 2016. https://www.theguardian.com/commentisfree/2016/oct/04/elena-ferrante-great-aunt-outed -henry-handel-richardson (accessed March 6, 2021).

Nichols, Catherine. "Homme de Plume: What I Learned Sending My Novel Out Under a Male Name." *Jezebel*. August 4, 2015. https://jezebel.com/homme-de-plume-what-i-learned-sending-my-novel-out -und-1720637627 (accessed March 6, 2021).

Novack, Kate. *Hysterical Girl*. Online documentary short. Distributed by the *New York Times*. 2020.

O'Connor, Kate. "The Anonymous Jane Austen." Writers Inspire. University of Oxford. July 11, 2012. http://writersinspire.org/content/anonymous-jane-austen (accessed April 2020).

Oliver, Sarah. "She Fought on the Somme Disguised as a Tommy, so Why Did Dorothy Die Unloved and Unlauded in a Lunatic Asylum? Incredible Story of the Only British Woman to Fight in the Trenches." *Daily Mail*. January 11, 2014. https://www.dailymail.co.uk/femail/article-2537793/She-fought-Somme-disguised -Tommy-did-Dorothy-die-unloved-unlauded-lunatic-asylum-Incredible-story-British-woman-fight-trenches. html (accessed May 7, 2020).

Osnos, Evan. "Thank You, Rusty Kanokogi." *New Yorker*. June 9, 2018. https://www.newyorker.com/news/ evan-osnos/thank-you-rusty-kanokogi (accessed March 7, 2021).

Oyler, Lauren. "It's Really Sickening How Much Florence Nightingale Hated Women." *Vice*. November 20, 2015. https://www.vice.com/en/article/kb4jd3/its-really-sickening-how-much-florence-nightingale-hated -women (accessed June 15, 2021).

Panja, Tariq. "Iranian Women Allowed to Attend Soccer Game for First Time Since 1981." *New York Times*. October 10, 2019. https://www.nytimes.com/2019/10/10/sports/soccer/iran-women.html?smid=tw-share (accessed March 7, 2021).

Pernoud, Régine. *Joan of Arc: By Herself and Her Witness*. Translated by Edward Hyams. Lanham, MD: Scarborough House, 1994.

Petry, Elisabeth. *At Home Inside: A Daughter's Tribute to Ann Petry*. Jackson: University of Mississippi, 2009.

Phillips, Julie. *James Tiptree, Jr.: The Double Life of Alice B. Sheldon.* New York: St. Martin's Press, 2006.

Platt, Charles. "Profile: James Tiptree, Jr." *Isaac Asimov's Science Fiction Magazine,* April 1983, 26–49.

Porter, Mary Jean. "Buffalo Gal: Notable Woman Soldier Lived in Pueblo." *Pueblo Chieftain.* https://www
.nmhistoricwomen.org/wp-content/uploads/2017/08/Williams-Cathay-additional-info.-pdf-compressed.pdf
(June 15, 2021).

"The Power of Ann Petry: 'The Issues . . . She Faces Resonate with Our Times.'" Library of America.
February 15, 2019. https://www.loa.org/news-and-views/1483-the-power-of-ann-petry-the-issues-she
-faces-resonate-with-our-times (accessed June 23, 2021).

Prelle, Monica. "When Bobbi Gibb Crashed the Boston Marathon and Blazed a Trail for Women." *Vice.* April
14, 2016. https://www.vice.com/en/article/9apy8z/when-bobbi-gibb-crashed-the-boston-marathon-and-
blazed-a-trail-for-women (accessed June 5, 2020).

"Q&A with Barbara McCaskill About Ellen and William Craft." News from the University of Georgia Press.
April 17, 2018. https://ugapress.wordpress.com/2018/04/17/qa-with-barbara-mccaskill-about-ellen-and
-william-craft/ (accessed February 6, 2020).

Rannard, Georgia, and BBC Monitoring. "World Cup 2018: Women Finally Allowed in Iranian Football
Stadium." BBC. June 21, 2018. bbc.com/news/blogs-trending-44561909 (accessed June 15, 2021).

Robinson, Joshua. "Judo Icon, a Fighter for Her Sport, Is Facing a New Battle." *New York Times.* February 16,
2009. https://www.nytimes.com/2009/02/17/sports/othersports/17judo.html (accessed June 9, 2018).

———. "Rusty Kanokogi, Fiery Advocate for Women's Judo, Dies at 74." *New York Times.* November 22,
2009. https://www.nytimes.com/2009/11/23/sports/olympics/23kanokogi.html (accessed June 9, 2018).

Rodger, Gillian M. *Just One of the Boys: Female-to-Male Cross-Dressing on the American Variety Stage.* Chicago:
University of Illinois Press, 2018.

Roehrig, Catharine, Renée Dreyfus, and Cathleen A. Keller, eds. *Hatshepsut: From Queen to Pharaoh.*
New Haven, CT: Yale University Press, 2005.

Rostenberg, Leona. "Some Anonymous and Pseudonymous Thrillers of Louisa M. Alcott." *Papers of the
Bibliographical Society of America* (University of Chicago Press) 37, no. 2 (1943): 131–40.

"Rumbling with Rusty." *Sports Illustrated.* March 24, 1986. https://vault.si.com/vault/1986/03/24/rumbling-rusty
(accessed June 9, 2018).

Ryan, Hugh. "Themstory: This Black Drag King Was Once Known as the Greatest Male Impersonator of All
Time." Them. June 1, 2018. https://www.them.us/story/themstory-florence-hines (accessed 12 June, 2020).

———. *When Brooklyn Was Queer: A History.* New York: St. Martin's Press, 2019.

Sampson, Fiona. "Frankenstein at 200—Why Hasn't Mary Shelley Been Given the Respect She Deserves?" *The Guardian*. January 13, 2018. https://www.theguardian.com/books/2018/jan/13/frankenstein-at-200-why -hasnt-mary-shelley-been-given-the-respect-she-deserves- (accessed April 14, 2020).

Segrave, Kerry. *Masquerading in Male Attire: Women Passing as Men in America, 1844–1920*. Jefferson, NC: McFarland & Company, Inc, 2018.

"The Six Who Sat." *30 for 30 Podcasts*. Season 4, episode 3. https://30for30podcasts.com/episodes/six-who -sat/ (accessed May 2020).

Slagle, Judith Bailey. "Joanna Baillie and the Anxiety of Shakespeare's Influence." *Borrowers and Lenders: The Journal of Shakespeare and Appropriation* (University of Georgia) 8, 1 (May 2013). https://openjournals .libs.uga.edu/borrowers/article/view/2203 (accessed June 22, 2021).

Smith, Alex Duval. "Solved at Last: The Burning Mystery of Joan of Arc." *The Guardian*. December 16, 2006. https://www.theguardian.com/world/2006/dec/17/france.alexduvalsmith (accessed August 4, 2018).

Souter, Anna. "The Dark Side of Surrealism that Exploited Women's 'Hysteria.'" Artsy. January 18, 2019. https://www.artsy.net/article/artsy-editorial-dark-side-surrealism-exploited-womens-hysteria (accessed July 17, 2020).

"Surprise! Harper Lee Is in Fact a Woman." *The Guardian*. February 3, 2015. https://www.theguardian.com/ books/2015/feb/03/surprise-harper-lee-is-a-woman (accessed March 26, 2020).

Switzer, Kathrine. *Marathon Woman*. New York: Da Capo Press, 2017.

Thompson, Patricia. "George Sand and English Reviewers: The First Twenty Years." *Modern Language Review* (Modern Humanities Research Association) 67, no. 3 (July 1972): 501–16.

Toler, Pamela D. *Women Warriors: An Unexpected History*. Boston: Beacon Press, 2019.

Toorpakai, Maria, and Katherine Holstein. *A Different Kind of Daughter: The Girl Who Hid from the Taliban in Plain Sight*. New York: Twelve, 2016.

Tucker, Phillip Thomas. *Anne Bonny the Infamous Female Pirate*. Port Townsend, WA: Feral House, 2017.

Wagner, Grace. "Durable and Elegant: Mary Edwards Walker and Dress Reform." *Special Collections Research Center* (blog), Syracuse University Libraries. June 9, 2020. https://library-blog.syr.edu/scrc/2020/06/09/ durable-and-elegant-mary-edwards-walker-and-dress-reform/ (accessed August 13, 2020).

Walker, Mary Edwards. *Hit*. New York: American News Company, 1871. Accessed at Google Books, August 13, 2019. https://www.google.com/books/edition/Hit/lyYdrMrnfjoC?hl=en&gbpv=0 (August 10, 2020).

Wallinger, Hanna. *Pauline E. Hopkins: A Literary Biography*. Athens: University of Georgia Press, 2005.

Watt, Ian. *The Rise of the Novel*. Updated ed. Berkeley: University of California Press, 2001.

"When Mary Shelley Met Lady Margaret." *Independent.ie*. December 3, 2017. https://www.independent.ie/
entertainment/books/when-mary-shelley-met-lady-margaret-36368448.html (accessed September 2, 2020).

Wilson, Elizabeth B. "The Queen Who Would Be King." *Smithsonian Magzine*. September 2006. https://www
.smithsonianmag.com/history/the-queen-who-would-be-king-130328511/ (accessed August 18, 2020).

Wirth, Robert, ed. "Primary Sources and Context Concerning Joan of Arc's Male Clothing." Joan of Arc:
Primary Sources Series. JoanofArcStudies.org. Translated by Allen Williamson. Historical Academy for Joan
of Arc Studies. 2006. http://primary-sources-series.joan-of-arc-studies.org/PSS021806.pdf (accessed February
2021).

"Women with a Past." BBC Radio Scotland. April 23, 2017. https://www.bbc.co.uk/programmes/b01nxw8h
(accessed June 23, 2021).

Woolf, Virginia. *A Room of One's Own*. Accessed at Project Gutenberg Australia, October 2002. http://
gutenberg.net.au/ebooks02/0200791.txt (June 16, 2021).

Yeoman, Louise. "The Woman Who Became a Witch-Pricker." BBC Scotland. November 18, 2012. https://
www.bbc.com/news/uk-scotland-20315106 (accessed August 2, 2018).

First published in 2022 by Harper Design
An Imprint of HarperCollins*Publishers*
195 Broadway
New York, NY 10007
Tel: (212) 207-7000
Fax: (855) 746-6023
harperdesign@harpercollins.com
hc.com

Distributed throughout the world by
HarperCollins*Publishers*
195 Broadway
New York, NY 10007

ISBN 978-0-06-306106-4

Library of Congress Control Number: 2021016255

Illustrations by Tina Berning
Design by What Studio?

Printed in Malaysia
First Printing, 2022

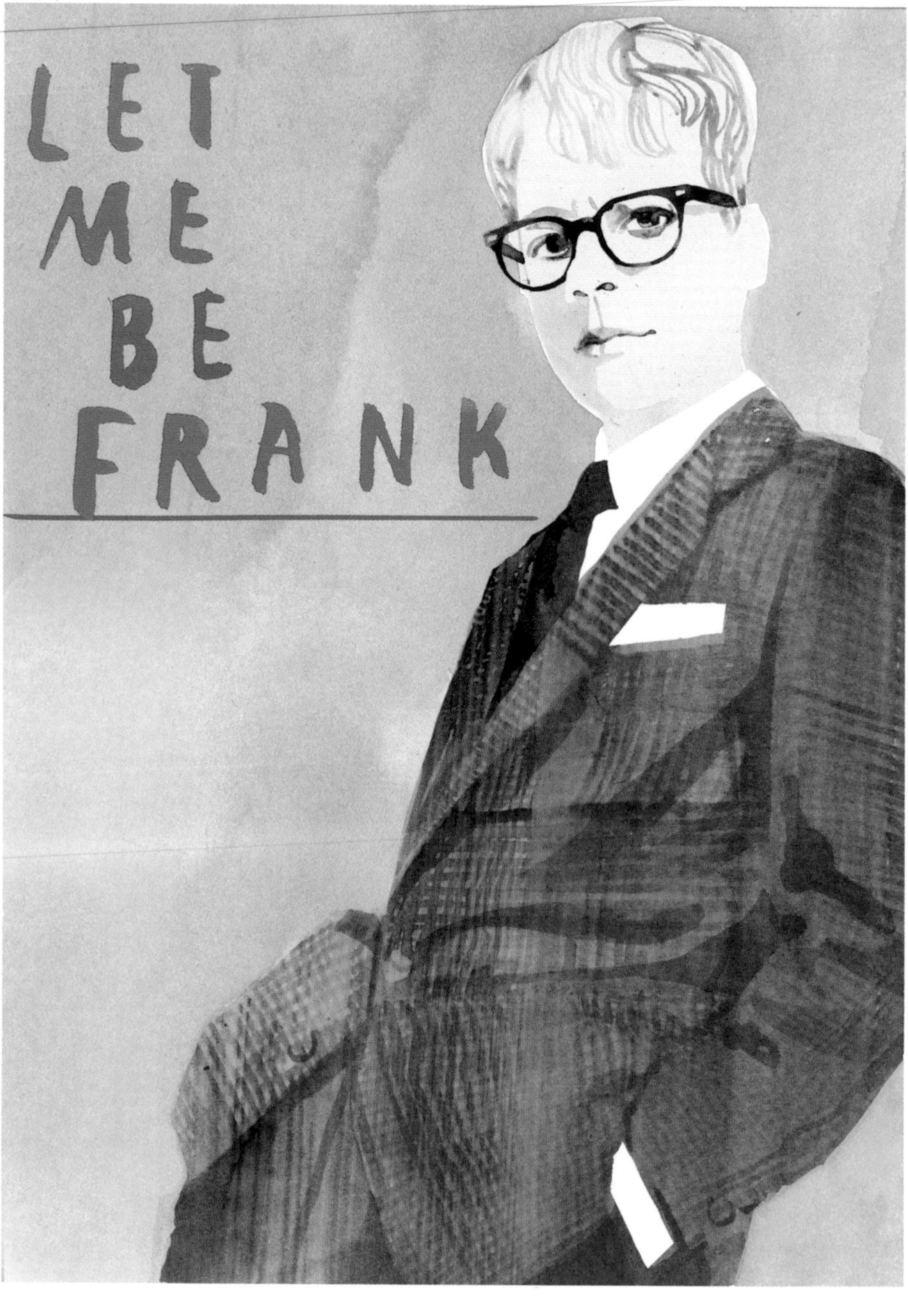
LET
ME
BE
FRANK

ABOUT THE AUTHOR

Canadian American writer and actor Tracy Dawson began her career on the main stage of the world-renowned Second City in Toronto. In 2009, Tracy won an emerging TV writer award at the Banff World Television Festival and soon after was staffed as a writer (and subsequently cast as a lead actor) on the television series *Call Me Fitz* (DirecTV, HBO Canada). Tracy went on to win the Gemini Award and the Canadian Screen Award for Best Lead Actress in a Comedy Series for her work as Jason Priestley's wildly problematic sister on *Fitz*.

In 2009, Tracy's play, *them & us*, was produced by the prestigious Theatre Passe Muraille in Toronto. Fans of Disney Channel Halloween movies will know Tracy from her portrayal of Deimata in *Girl vs. Monster*. In 2014, Tracy wrote on the TBS sitcom, *Your Family or Mine*, where she got to write jokes for Richard Dreyfuss and Ed Begley Jr. Ed called her a genius once. I'm just saying. Tracy has acted in countless projects on stage and screen and has sold several television projects, both in the US and in Canada. She was born in Ottawa, Canada, and currently lives in Los Angeles with her life partner, Isaac, who is a dog. *Let Me Be Frank* is her first book.

 @dawsontracy